P9-DCE-339

This book belongs to

____

Given by _______________________

Date ____________________

The One Year® DEVOTIONS for Preschoolers

Written by Crystal Bowman
Illustrated by Elena Kucharik

Tyndale House Publishers, Inc.
CAROL STREAM, ILLINOIS

Visit Tyndale's website for kids at www.tyndale.com/kids.

The One Year Devotions for Preschoolers

Edited by Betty Free Swanberg
Designed by Alyssa Force

For manufacturing information regarding this product, please call 1-800-323-9400.

The Library of Congress has catalogued the first edition as follows:

Bowman, Crystal.
The one year book of devotions for preschoolers / written by Crystal Bowman; illustrated by Elena Kucharik.
p. cm.
ISBN 978-0-8423-8940-2 (hc)
1. Preschool children—Prayer-books and devotions—English. 2. Devotional calendars—Juvenile literature. I. Kucharik, Elena. II. Title.
BV4870.B64 2004
242'.62—dc22 2004002325

Printed in China

19 18 17 16 15
17 16 15 14

January

1
JANUARY

Happy Faces

Jack likes to play outdoors. He thinks winter is lots of fun. Jack made a great big snowman and put a happy smile on the snowman's face. Are you wearing a happy smile today? A smile on the outside means that you are happy on the inside. God gives us many reasons to be happy. He loves us. He cares for us. And he is our friend. God can help us be happy inside and out.

My Bible Verse:
A happy heart makes a face look cheerful. Proverbs 15:13, NIrV

My Prayer:
Help me, God, to be happy today
As I work and as I play.

Practice, Practice, Practice!

2 JANUARY

Zoë likes to learn new things. She is learning to play her violin, but sometimes it's hard to do. Do you think she should keep practicing? If she does, she can learn to play a new song. God created us so we can learn new things. And he promises to help us when we try. There are many things that are fun to learn, but everything takes practice. Do you want to ride a bike or hit a baseball or play the piano? You can learn to do many things if you practice, practice, practice!

My Bible Verse:
I can do everything with the help of Christ who gives me the strength I need. Philippians 4:13, NLT

My Prayer:
When I'm learning something new, Lord, I get my strength from you.

3 JANUARY

When I Grow Up

Parker wants to be a doctor when he grows up. Do you know what you want to be? You might like to be an artist, a nurse, an astronaut, or maybe a police officer. God has good plans for you. He knows what you will enjoy doing someday. And he will help you be good at doing it. If you pray to God and learn what he says in the Bible, he will help you know what he wants you to be.

My Bible Verse:
Seek his will in all you do,
and he will direct your paths.
Proverbs 3:6, NLT

My Prayer:
Show me, God, so I can see
Exactly what you want me to be.

A Special Place

4 JANUARY

Kaitlyn made her very own house where she can work and play. It's fun to have a special place that's just for you. Did you know that God is making a special place for you in heaven? He has given you a special place to live on earth right now. You will probably live here for a long time. But someday you will live in a VERY special place in heaven that God made just for you. And you will live there for a VERY long time—forever and ever!

My Bible Verse:

There are many rooms in my Father's house. . . . I am going there to prepare a place for you.
John 14:2, ICB

My Prayer:

Someday, Lord, I will see your face
And live in a very special place!

5 JANUARY

Angels Everywhere

Did you ever make angels in the snow? The Bible tells us there are real angels who live with God in heaven. But did you know that there are angels who live with us right here on earth? Even though we can't see them, God's angels are all around us every day. God tells them to take care of us and keep us safe wherever we go.

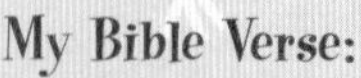

My Bible Verse:

The Lord will command his angels to take good care of you. Psalm 91:11, NIrV

My Prayer:

Thank you for angels everywhere
Who always keep me in their care.

Animals Big and Small

6
JANUARY

Do you have a pet in your house? Maybe you have a dog or a cat or a fish. Pets need water and food just like we do. Do you give your pet food and water? If you don't have a pet, maybe you can feed the birds or bunnies in your yard. God created lots of animals for us to enjoy. God is happy when we take care of the animals he made.

My Bible Verse:
All the animals of the forest are mine. Psalm 50:10, NLT

My Prayer:
Thank you for animals big and small.
Dear God, I know you made them all.

7

JANUARY

Think and Learn

Kids like you have lots of questions. What are some questions you have? Maybe you wonder: Where do clouds come from? Why does it rain? How big are the mountains? What makes the wind blow? God gave each of us a mind so we can think and learn about many things. But no matter how many answers we find or how much we learn, we will never know as much as God does. God knows more than anyone could ever imagine.

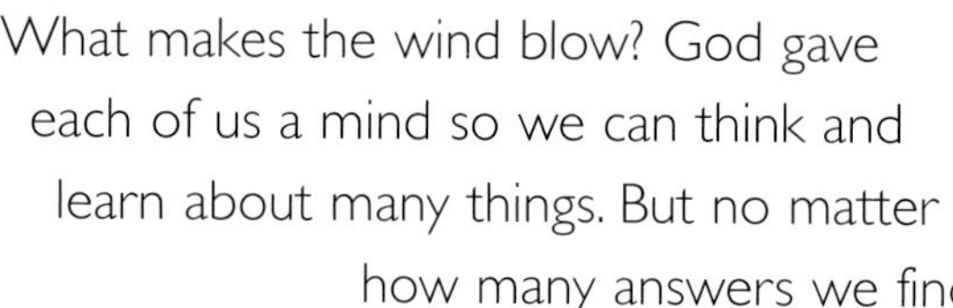

My Bible Verse:

God's wisdom and knowledge have no end! Romans 11:33, ICB

My Prayer:

Lord, please help my mind to grow. Teach me all I need to know.

God Will Listen

8

JANUARY

Parker needs someone to talk to, so he is going to talk to God. He is going to pray. Did you know that you can talk to God anytime of the day or night? God is always ready to listen to your prayers no matter where you are or what you are doing. Sometimes Mom and Dad are both busy. And sometimes friends aren't around. But God will listen when you need to talk—in the morning, in the afternoon, and all through the night.

My Bible Verse:

Pray to me, and I will answer you. Jeremiah 33:3, ICB

My Prayer:

Lord, I know that I can pray
Anytime of the night or day.

9
JANUARY

What Day Is It?

What if it never got dark? You wouldn't know when to play and when to sleep. That's why God created the sun for the day and the moon for the night. The sun and moon help us to know when it's a new day. One-two-three-four-five-six-seven days and nights make a week. And 52 weeks make each of us a whole year older! The sun and moon also help us keep track of the seasons—spring and summer and fall and winter.

My Bible Verse:

Let bright lights appear in the sky to separate the day from the night. They will be signs to mark off the seasons, the days, and the years.
Genesis 1:14, NLT

My Prayer:

Dear God, you made the day and night,
The sun and moon to give us light.

No More Fighting!

10 JANUARY

Zoë and Kaitlyn are fighting. Sometimes friends get mad and argue when something bad happens between them. God doesn't want us to yell and fight. He knows that will make us feel worse. God wants us to talk about what happened instead. Talking is better than fighting because it will make us feel better inside. Zoë and Kaitlyn talked about what happened. Then they stopped fighting. And now they are friends again.

My Bible Verse:
Because you belong to the Lord, settle your disagreement.
Philippians 4:2, NLT

My Prayer:
Help me, Lord, to do what is right,
To talk things out instead of fight.

11

JANUARY

King of the Earth

It's a cold winter day where Jack lives. He is wearing a warm jacket and hat and mittens and boots. He is watching snowflakes fall down from the sky. God created those soft, tiny snowflakes. But God also created the huge mountains, the tall trees, and the big, deep oceans. Isn't that amazing? God is the only one who is great enough to create all these things. Since God made everything, he is the King of the earth. Can you think of some other things that God made?

My Bible Verse:

How awesome is the Lord Most High, the great King over all the earth! Psalm 47:2, NIV

My Prayer:

Oh, Lord, you are my God and King,
Maker and ruler of everything.

Don't Worry

12 JANUARY

Oh, no! Kaitlyn lost her baby kittens! She is worried that something bad will happen to them. But God tells us in the Bible that we do not need to worry about anything. God wants us to pray to him instead of worrying. When we tell God about our problems, he helps us. If Kaitlyn prays, how might God help her?

My Bible Verse:

Do not worry about anything. But pray and ask God for everything you need.
Philippians 4:6, ICB

My Prayer:

Dear God, I know it's best to pray.
So help me not to worry today.

13

JANUARY

Happy Helpers

Jack and his friends are cleaning their church. How do you help at your church? How do you help at home? Everyone needs to be a helper when there is work to be done. Whether we work or play, God wants us to do it to please him. He wants us to be thankful that we are able to work. So the next time you need to be a helper, tell God thank you and do your work for him.

My Bible Verse:

Do everything you say or do in the name of the Lord Jesus. Always give thanks to God the Father through Christ. Colossians 3:17, NIrV

My Prayer:

Lord, I want to do my part.
Help me to work with a thankful heart.

Happy Friends

14
JANUARY

Parker and Jack like doing things together. God created us so that we need each other. God is happy when people help each other and are kind to one another. God wants us to play nicely with our friends. God wants us to be kind to the people in our neighborhood. And God especially wants us to love everyone who loves him. Can you think of something kind you can do for someone today?

My Bible Verse:

How good and pleasant it is when God's people live together in peace! Psalm 133:1, NIrV

My Prayer:

Help me, dear God, to be kind and good
And always treat others the way that I should.

15 JANUARY

Obey Your Parents

Jack's parents told him not to touch the cookie jar. But he did, and it broke. Maybe your parents have rules like: Don't touch the stove. Don't cross the street. No cookies before dinner. Your parents make rules because they love you and they know what is best for you. They want to protect you and keep you healthy and safe. God wants you to obey your parents. When you do, you are also obeying God.

My Bible Verse:

Children, obey your parents the way the Lord wants. This is theright thing to do.
Ephesians 6:1, ICB

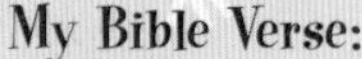

My Prayer:

Help me, Jesus, to obey
And do what's right all through the day.

Feet That Follow

16
JANUARY

Parker and Zoë are putting new shoes on their feet. Do you think their feet will take them out to play? Will their feet take them to the store? Maybe their feet will take them to church. The Bible tells us to walk with God. You can walk with him by doing the things that he wants you to do. When you obey God and do what is right, you are following in his footsteps.

My Bible Verse:
Walk in all the way that the Lord your God has commanded you.
Deuteronomy 5:33, NIV

My Prayer:
Dear God, in everything I do I want to take each step with you.

17

JANUARY

Always Be Thankful

Kaitlyn and Zoë are making a big mess! But after they clean it up, everything will be okay. Sometimes we have problems in our lives that seem like big messes. Things don't always go the way we want them to. But do you know what? God wants us to be thankful anyway. He can make our big messes turn out okay.

My Bible Verse:

No matter what happens, always be thankful, for this is God's will for you who belong to Christ Jesus.
1 Thessalonians 5:18, NLT

My Prayer:

When things don't always go my way,
Please help me know it will be okay.

Don't Be Afraid

18 JANUARY

Poor Jack! He heard a noise and now he is afraid. It was only a little mouse that wouldn't hurt him, but Jack didn't know that. Do you ever feel afraid? Everybody feels afraid now and then. But God doesn't want us to stay feeling that way. God wants us to remember that he will always take care of us. If we believe God's promises, then we don't need to be afraid.

My Bible Verse:
God has come to save me. I will trust in him and not be afraid.
Isaiah 12:2, NLT

My Prayer:
When I'm afraid, here's what I'll do—
God, I will put my trust in you.

19

JANUARY

Share the Good News!

Have you ever met a missionary? That's someone who tells other people the Good News about God and his Son, Jesus. Sometimes missionaries travel to countries that are far away. The children in this picture are looking at a globe. It shows where all of the different countries are. Missionaries work very hard. It is important to pray for missionaries so more people can learn about God. Maybe someday you will be a missionary too.

My Bible Verse:

What a beautiful sight it is to see messengers coming with good news! Isaiah 52:7, NIrV

My Prayer:

Bless the missionaries far, far away. Help them know all the right words to say.

Hungry Tummies

Look at all the good food to eat! What is your favorite food? Is it pizza? Is it popcorn? Maybe it's sweet, juicy apples. People need food to eat and water to drink every day. Food and water help to make us healthy and strong. Everything we eat and drink comes from the world that God made. When you eat a meal or a snack and have something good to drink, remember to say thank you to God.

My Bible Verse:
He satisfies the thirsty and fills the hungry with good things.
Psalm 107:9, NLT

My Prayer:
Thank you for food and water, too.
Lord, these blessings come from you.

21 JANUARY

Important People

Do you ever get dressed up and pretend you are someone very important? Maybe you like to pretend you're a beautiful princess or a handsome prince. It's fun to pretend. But do you know what? You don't have to pretend, because you are important! When you love Jesus with all your heart, God is your Father and you are his child. And since God is the King, you are a child of a king. That makes you a real prince or princess!

My Bible Verse:

And since we are his children, we will share his treasures.
Romans 8:17, NLT

My Prayer:

Oh, God, you are my Father above.
Thank you for giving me all of your love.

Too Many to Count!

22 JANUARY

Kaitlyn has pretty hair. What color is it? What color is your hair? Do you think Kaitlyn can count all the hairs on her head? Of course not! It's impossible to count the hairs on your head. But it's not impossible for God. The Bible says that God knows everything about you from your head to your toes. He even knows how many hairs you have on your head! Go ahead—see how many of them you can count!

My Bible Verse:
He even counts every hair on your head! Matthew 10:30, NIrV

My Prayer:
Dear God, I'm amazed at what you know.
You know all about me, from head to toe.

23

JANUARY

Giving and Receiving

Jack and Zoë are giving birthday presents to Kaitlyn. What do you think might be inside the boxes? It's fun to open a pretty package and find out what's inside. But it can also be fun to give a present to someone else. When you give someone a gift, it makes the person feel happy and special. And that should make you feel happy and special too! Jesus says that it's even better to give than to receive. So whether a gift is for you or for someone else, you can be happy.

My Bible Verse:

Remember the words of the Lord Jesus: "It is more blessed to give than to receive." Acts 20:35, NLT

My Prayer:

Jesus, I will be happy to give,
'Cause that's the way you want
me to live.

A Strong House

24 JANUARY

It's fun to play outdoors. But you probably wouldn't want to live outside. If you get cold, you can run home to get warm. Aren't you happy you have a place to live that keeps you warm? Our homes are strong too. They keep us safe on windy days and stormy nights. But God is stronger than any building. When we believe in God and do what he says in the Bible, he promises to keep us safe.

My Bible Verse:

The Lord is like a strong tower. Those who do what is right can run to him for safety.
Proverbs 18:10, ICB

My Prayer:

Oh, Lord, there is nothing stronger than you.
Please keep me safe in all that I do.

25
JANUARY

Busy Days

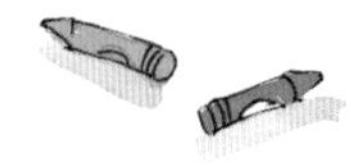

What are you going to do today? Will you read some books? Will you color pictures or play with friends? There are so many things to do that sometimes it's hard to choose. It's important to play. It's important to help others. It's important to learn. It's important to rest. But it is most important to do what Kaitlyn is doing. She is reading the Bible and learning how to talk to God.

My Bible Verse:
Remember your Creator while you are young. Ecclesiastes 12:1, ICB

My Prayer:
Thank you that I can learn and play. Bless me in all that I do today.

The Shepherd and His Sheep

Do you see the toy sheep? Real sheep never have to worry. Do you know why? It's because a person called a shepherd takes care of them. If the sheep need food, the shepherd leads them to a place where they can eat. If the sheep are tired, the shepherd watches over them while they sleep. If one sheep gets lost, the shepherd finds it. The Bible says that God is our Shepherd and we are his sheep. He loves us and takes care of us just like a shepherd takes care of his sheep.

My Bible Verse:

The Lord is my shepherd; I have everything I need. Psalm 23:1, NLT

My Prayer:

You are my Shepherd and I am your sheep.
You give me food and a safe place to sleep.

27
JANUARY

Tell Me a Story

Everyone is listening to Zoë. She is telling a story from the Bible. Do you like to listen to stories? Jesus told lots of stories called parables, and they're in the Bible. Jesus told the parables to help people understand more about God and his love. Big crowds of people would follow Jesus just to hear his stories. Even though he told them a long time ago, we can still listen to them today.

My Bible Verse:
I will speak to you in parables.
I will explain mysteries hidden since the creation of the world.
Matthew 13:35, NLT

My Prayer:
Thank you for stories, old and new,
That help me learn so much about you.

Doing Good

28
JANUARY

Jack feeds his dog every day. What are some things you do every day? Do you make your bed every day? Do you brush your teeth every day? Do you feed your pet every day?

Sometimes we get tired of doing things over and over again. It's not that those things really make us tired—it's just that we don't like having to do them so often. We feel like giving up. But there is one thing that we must never give up. That is doing good things for others. Jesus wants us to help people over and over again.

My Bible Verse:
Don't get tired of doing what is good. Don't get discouraged and give up. Galatians 6:9, NLT

My Prayer:
Help me to do the things that I should
And never get tired of doing good.

29 JANUARY

Lots of Guests

Kaitlyn invited her friends over for lunch. Can you count how many people there are at the table? It looks like there are four people, but do you know what? There is someone else at the table that you can't see. Jesus says that if two or more of his children come together to pray or talk about him, he is there too. Jesus likes to be with you and your friends when you get together.

My Bible Verse:

If two or three people come together in my name, I am there with them. Matthew 18:20, ICB

My Prayer:

Jesus, I know you will always be
Right here with all of my friends
and me.

Nobody's Perfect!

30
JANUARY

The puppy knocked over a pot of dirt and made a big mess for Kaitlyn. He feels sad, because he tries to be good. Do you try to be good? Of course you do! But no matter how hard we try, sometimes we do things we should not do. When we do something wrong, we need to tell God that we're sorry. Because God loves us, he will forgive us. And he will help us do our best every day.

My Bible Verse:
With all my heart I try to obey you, God. Don't let me break your commands. Psalm 119:10, ICB

My Prayer:
I'm sorry, God, for the things I do
That do not please and honor you.

31 JANUARY

Good Night! Sleep Tight!

Zoë is ready to sleep. She likes her big, fluffy pillow and her soft, warm blanket. Zoë feels safe in her cozy bed. She knows that God stays awake all night and watches over her. Do you feel safe in your bed at night? Even if everyone in the whole house is sleeping, God is still awake. God doesn't get tired like we do. God watches over you every night so you can sleep tight.

My Bible Verse:
The one who watches over you will not sleep. Psalm 121:3, NLT

My Prayer:
Lord, you watch me sleep each night.
Keep me safe till the morning light.

February

1 FEBRUARY

Quiet Places

The birds are sleeping. The neighborhood is quiet. Parker is in his backyard, looking at the sky. He likes to look at the moon and the twinkling stars. The lights in the sky make him think about how great God is. When we are busy playing and talking, we think about a lot of things. But when it's quiet, it is easier to think about God. Can you find a quiet place and think about God?

My Bible Verse:
Be still, and know that I am God.
Psalm 46:10, NIV

My Prayer:
Quiet places are sometimes the best
To think about you and know I am
blessed.

Forget about It

2 FEBRUARY

Oh, no! Kaitlyn's cat messed up Jack's picture! Jack doesn't look very happy. Did a pet or a friend ever mess up your picture or break one of your toys? Did you get mad? It's easy to become angry when things like that happen. But do you know what? If you really love someone, you'll forget about it and stop being mad. You'll just make a new picture or play with another toy. And your friend will still be your friend.

My Bible Verse:

Love is patient. . . . It does not easily become angry. It does not keep track of other people's wrongs. 1 Corinthians 13:4-5, NIrV

My Prayer:

Help me, God, to forgive and forget,
To love my friends and not get upset.

3 FEBRUARY

Powerful Words

Do you like to make things? When you build something, you use your hands, don't you? But look at the world God made. All he had to do to make it was talk! God is so powerful that whatever he says just happens. When God said, "Let there be light!" there was light. God created the whole world that way. He made the trees. He made the mountains. He made the oceans. And he made all the animals. He did it just by saying the words.

My Bible Verse:

The Lord merely spoke, and the heavens were created. He breathed the word, and all the stars were born. Psalm 33:6, NLT

My Prayer:

Dear God, you're great! You said the words
To make the mountains and the birds.

Take a Rest

4
FEBRUARY

Zoë says it's time for a nap. Do you ever get so tired that you just can't stay awake? Sometimes we get tired because we need to sleep. People can also get tired when they have a lot of problems. Thinking about problems all day long can make us feel tired and sad. Jesus wants us to talk to him about our problems. He can help us. When we share our problems with Jesus, it's like taking a nap.

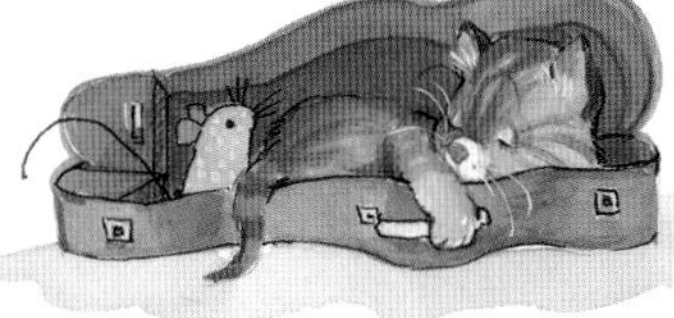

My Bible Verse:
Come to me, all of you who are tired and have heavy loads. I will give you rest. Matthew 11:28, ICB

My Prayer:
Thank you, Jesus, for giving me rest. Talking to you is always the best.

5 FEBRUARY

Listen Up!

Jack is telling his animal friends about things he has been learning. Children have many things to learn. That's why God gives you parents and grandparents and teachers to teach you how to live. If you listen to them, you will grow up to be very wise. Then you can teach important things to your children someday.

My Bible Verse:
Get all the advice and instruction you can, and be wise the rest of your life. Proverbs 19:20, NLT

My Prayer:
Help me, Lord, to listen today
To words that grown-ups have to say.

In God's Image

Kaitlyn looks at herself in the mirror and sees her image. It looks just like her! When God created the world, he made the sun and the moon. He made the flowers and the trees. And he made all the animals. But when God created people, he made us in his image. That means we're a lot like him, even though he doesn't have a body. We can think like God. We can be happy or sad like him. And we can talk to God. People are more important than anything else God created.

My Bible Verse:
God created people in his own image; God patterned them after himself. Genesis 1:27, NLT

My Prayer:
Thank you for making me just like you,
So I can pray and be happy, too.

7 FEBRUARY

A Special Book

Kaitlyn is looking at a special book full of pictures. The pictures are of Kaitlyn's family and friends. Kaitlyn's special book makes her feel happy. Did you know that God has a special book too? His book has names in it. When people believe in Jesus, God writes their names in the special book. God is happy when he can write someone's name in his special book.

My Bible Verse:

I will never erase their names from the Book of Life.
Revelation 3:5, NLT

My Prayer:

Dear Jesus, I believe in you.
I want my name in your book too.

Amazing and Wonderful

8 FEBRUARY

Zoë and Parker are using their legs to walk through the woods. They are using their arms to carry a bird and a bunny. And Zoë is pulling her big dog in a little wagon! Do you like to walk and climb and run? Do you like to carry things? Maybe you like to use your tongue to lick an ice cream cone. Isn't it nice to feel the softness of a kitten and to splash in a pool? You can say thank you to God for creating you to do many things.

My Bible Verse:

How you made me is amazing and wonderful. I praise you for that. What you have done is wonderful. I know that very well.

Psalm 139:14, NIrV

My Prayer:

I praise you, God, for all I can do. I'm special and blessed—I'm created by you.

9 FEBRUARY

Bumps and Bruises

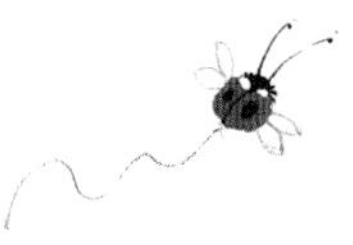

Jack has a bump on his knee. He is wrapping a bandage around it so it will feel better. God can heal Jack's knee and make the bump go away. But did you know that you can get bumps and bruises on the inside, too? When something bad happens to you or to someone you love, you feel sad and hurt. It's hard for you to fix the hurts on the inside. But God loves you very much. He can heal you on the inside and on the outside.

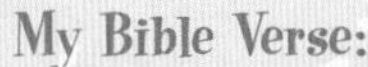

My Bible Verse:

He heals the brokenhearted.
He bandages their wounds.
Psalm 147:3, ICB

My Prayer:

Lord, you heal me inside and out.
It makes me want to jump and shout!

What to Wear!

10 FEBRUARY

Zoë doesn't know what to wear today. She wants to be warm and comfortable. And she doesn't want to wear the same thing she wore yesterday. Do you ever have a hard time deciding what to wear? There is nothing wrong with wondering what to wear. But God wants us to think about things that are even more important. Telling our friends about Jesus is more important than our clothes. If we spend our time on important things, then God will take care of everything else.

My Bible Verse:

The thing you should want most is God's kingdom and doing what God wants. Then all these other things you need will be given to you. Matthew 6:33, ICB

My Prayer:

Help me to please you in thought
and deed,
For then you will give me all that
I need.

11 FEBRUARY

Good Books

Jack is taking a Bible storybook down from a bookshelf. Do you like to look at books? You can learn about animals and people and spaceships. Books teach us many different things. But we can learn the most from reading the Bible. The Bible tells about things that happened a long time ago. And the Bible tells about things that will help us each day. There are many good books, but the Bible is the best of all!

My Bible Verse:

How I love your teachings!
I think about them all day long.
Psalm 119:97, ICB

My Prayer:

Thank you for the words you give.
They help me learn how I should live.

A Reward for You

12 FEBRUARY

Zoë won a trophy for being the best catcher on her baseball team. Have you ever won a prize for something you've done? People like winning prizes. Did you know that God has prizes for people who love and obey him? God's prizes are called rewards. Someday when we go to heaven, God will reward us for all the good things we have done.

My Bible Verse:

Remember that the Lord will reward each one of us for the good we do. Ephesians 6:8, NLT

My Prayer:

Help me to love and obey you,
dear Lord,
So I will receive my heavenly
reward.

13 FEBRUARY

Welcome Others

Jack told Kaitlyn he needs a place to stay. She is inviting him into her tree house. She will give him something to eat and let him rest. Has a friend or relative ever stayed at your home? God wants us to share our home with others. Sharing our home is a way to show God that we love him. Maybe you can show God you love him by sharing your room with a friend.

My Bible Verse:
Share with God's people who are in need. Welcome others into your homes. Romans 12:13, NIrV

My Prayer:
Jesus, help me to share my home
When someone's hungry and all alone.

Lots of Love

14
FEBRUARY

Jack loves his big stuffed lion. He loves his dog. He loves his family. And he loves all of his friends. Jack has a lot of love to share! Who do you love? Love is a wonderful gift that God has given us. We are able to love others because of God's love for us. God's love is big enough for everyone. Remember to thank God today for his gift of love.

My Bible Verse:

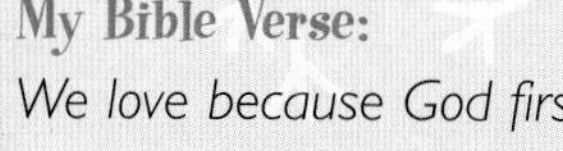

We love because God first loved us. 1 *John 4:19,* ICB

My Prayer:

Thank you, God, for loving me
So I can love my family.

15 FEBRUARY

Helping

Look at all of the helpers. What are some of the ways you like to help others? When you love Jesus, God helps you to be good at doing things for others. He helps some people to be good at giving. Some people are good at being helpers. Some people are good at teaching or being leaders. Some are good at making people happy. God wants you to use the abilities he gives you to help others.

My Bible Verse:

God has given each of us the ability to do certain things well.
Romans 12:6, NLT

My Prayer:

Help me to do what I can for others—
My parents, my sisters, and my brothers.

God Is Great

16
FEBRUARY

Parker is watching the sun set over the mountains. Have you ever looked up at a tall mountain? Have you ever watched a beautiful sunset? Have you ever seen the ocean or a big lake? God created these awesome things. Even though we can't see God, we can see how great he is by the wonderful things he has created. God is greater than everything he created.

My Bible Verse:

How great is the Lord, and how much we should praise him!
Psalm 48:1, NLT

My Prayer:

Dear God, you are great in so many ways!
I want to give you all of my praise.

17 FEBRUARY

Have Fun!

Parker is dressed up like a clown. Have you ever dressed up like a clown? It's fun to dress up and be silly. Someday when you grow up, you will have to work and take care of many things. Then you will remember how much fun it was to be young. God created you to be a child for a little while. When you grow up, you will be a grown-up the rest of your life. So have lots of fun while you are young!

My Bible Verse:

Young people, enjoy yourselves while you are young. Be happy while you are young.
Ecclesiastes 11:9, ICB

My Prayer:

I'm young for just a little while—
I love to laugh and love to smile!

Smart Animals

18
FEBRUARY

Did you know that animals are very smart? Birds know when it's time to fly south for the winter. Squirrels know how to hide acorns away for a snowy day. Some animals even dig holes in the ground so they can stay safe and warm. God created animals and made them smart so they would know how to take care of themselves. That's because God loves the animals he created.

My Bible Verse:
The life of every living thing is in his hand. Job 12:10, NLT

My Prayer:
You made the animals big and small. Please protect and love them all.

19

FEBRUARY

Staying Close

Zoë and the cat are afraid of the neighbor's big dog. When Zoë holds the cat in her arms, they both feel safe. What are you afraid of? Do you feel safe when someone you love is close by? The Bible tells us that God is always right beside us. When we are afraid, we can pray. Then we'll know God is protecting us. It will be just as if Jesus is holding us in his arms.

My Bible Verse:

I will not be afraid, for you are close beside me. Psalm 23:4, NLT

My Prayer:

Dear God, I know you are always near. Help me not to worry or fear.

Imitate God

20 FEBRUARY

Jack sees his shadow and tries to look like a bird. Do you ever flap your arms and pretend you are a bird flying in the air? Do you ever crawl on your hands and knees and roar like a hungry lion? Do you ever try to act just like your mom or dad? The Bible tells us to be just like God. Since God loves everyone, we can be like God by doing kind, loving things for others.

My Bible Verse:

You are the children that God dearly loves. So be just like him.
Ephesians 5:1, NIrV

My Prayer:

God, this is what I want to do—
I want to be a lot like you.

21 FEBRUARY

A Ruler Forever

When a person becomes the ruler of a country, he usually is the leader for just a few years. Then the people of the country vote for a new ruler. Even in Bible times many different kings ruled the land. Today some countries have a president and some countries have a king or queen. But God is the ruler over everyone. And he will be the ruler forever and ever.

My Bible Verse:

He is the living God, and he will endure forever. His kingdom will never be destroyed, and his rule will never end. Daniel 6:26, NLT

My Prayer:

Oh, Lord, you rule over all the land. Your kingdom will forever stand.

Great Things

22

FEBRUARY

How can you tell that the children in this picture are happy? How do you show that you are happy? God does wonderful things for us that give us a special kind of happiness called joy. He gives you a place to live and people to love you. He gives you food and water. He gives you toys and helps you talk and sing and laugh. So be happy and filled with joy! What other great things has God given you?

My Bible Verse:

The Lord has done great things for us, and we are filled with joy.
Psalm 126:3, NIV

My Prayer:

Dear God, you give me everything—
Like food to eat and songs to sing.

23 FEBRUARY

Be Generous

One for Parker, one for Jack. Two for Parker, two for Jack. The boys are sharing cookies. If they are generous, they will save some for Zoë and Kaitlyn too. A generous person gives more than what others expect to get. If someone wants one cookie and you give him two, that is being generous. How can you be generous today?

My Bible Verse:

Command them to do good, to be rich in good deeds, and to be generous and willing to share.
1 Timothy 6:18, NIV

My Prayer:

Help me, Lord, to always share
And send your blessings everywhere.

Wise and Safe

24 FEBRUARY

Kaitlyn and Jack are very wise. They are crossing the street together and watching out for cars. There are many wise things that children can do. It is wise to wear a seat belt in the car. It is wise to stay close to your mom in a store. Being wise keeps us safe. Can you think of other wise things you can do? If we do what God tells us in the Bible, we will be wise and safe.

My Bible Verse:
Those who walk in wisdom are safe. Proverbs 28:26, NLT

My Prayer:
Dear God, my wisdom comes from you. Keep me safe in all I do.

25
FEBRUARY

Great Big Hugs

Zoë loves her fluffy sheepdog. She is giving him a great big hug. Do you think she will hug the people in her family too? Who do you like to hug? When you hug other people, it makes you feel warm inside. And it helps others know that you love them. Giving someone a hug is like saying, "I love you!" without using words. How many people do you think you can hug today?

My Bible Verse:
I command you to love each other. John 15:17, NLT

My Prayer:
Help me to love my family today,
With lots of hugs and kind words to say.

Don't Stay Mad

26 FEBRUARY

Jack is mad. He is having a temper tantrum because he's angry about something that happened. Do you ever get mad? Everyone gets mad once in a while. The important thing is that we shouldn't stay feeling that way. The Bible tells us that by the end of the day, we should not be angry anymore. If you ever get mad, you can go to your room and rest for a while. You can sing a song. And you can ask Jesus to help you be happy and kind again.

My Bible Verse:

Do not go on being angry all day. Ephesians 4:26, ICB

My Prayer:

Help me, Jesus, when I am mad.
You're the one who can make me glad.

27 FEBRUARY

Cozy Comfort

Zoë likes to take care of her animals. She tucks them in bed and comforts them. Does someone tuck you in your bed at night? That feels good, doesn't it? The Bible says that God will take care of you just like a mother takes care of her children. That's because God is like a parent who loves you very much!

My Bible Verse:
As a mother comforts her child, so will I comfort you.
Isaiah 66:13, NIV

My Prayer:
You are my Father in heaven above.
Thank you for your comfort and your love.

Hide and Seek

28 FEBRUARY

Parker is playing hide-and-seek with his friends. Do you think he can find Zoë and Jack? Have you ever played hide-and-seek? When you hide behind a tree or a big bush, your friends can't see you—especially if it's dark! But God can always see you no matter where you are. Whether it's late at night or the middle of the day, God knows exactly where you are. You can never hide from God. He will always love you and take care of you.

My Bible Verse:

Even in darkness I cannot hide from you. Psalm 139:12, NLT

My Prayer:

Lord, I'm always in your sight—
When it's dark and when it's light.

29 FEBRUARY

Just Because

Jack is jumping because he is happy. It isn't his birthday. And he doesn't even have friends to play with today. So why is Jack happy? He is happy just because God loves him. You don't need lots of friends or special days to be happy. You can be happy because you're alive and you're able to enjoy God's world. You can be happy just because God loves you. Even if you think you're alone, you're not—God is there with you!

My Bible Verse:
Let the godly rejoice. Let them be glad in God's presence.
Psalm 68:3, NLT

My Prayer:
Dear God, I'm happy as can be,
Because of your great love for me.

March

1
MARCH

Sad Days

Parker is sad. A friend is going away on a train. Did one of your friends ever move to another neighborhood? Maybe you were the one who had to move away and leave friends behind. When you are sad, you can pray. You can ask God to make you feel better. God wants you to talk to him when you are sad. He is a good listener.

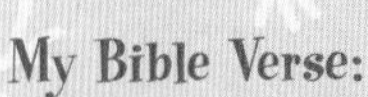

My Bible Verse:

The Lord and King will wipe away the tears from everyone's face.
Isaiah 25:8, NIrV

My Prayer:

You listen to me when I am sad.
You dry my tears and make me glad.

It Takes Time

2
MARCH

Zoë is telling God that she is glad to be growing up and learning how to do many things. But sometimes being young can be hard. Have you ever wished you were bigger or stronger or smarter? It takes many years to grow up. The important thing is to be happy that you are just who God wants you to be right now. God will help you grow and learn each day.

My Bible Verse:
God has made everything beautiful for its own time.
Ecclesiastes 3:11, NLT

My Prayer:
Remind me, God, and help me know—
It takes many years to learn and grow.

3
MARCH

Extra Help

Sometimes Kaitlyn and Jack have to do things they don't feel like doing. How about you? Would you rather play outdoors than set the table? Do you complain when your parents tell you it's time for bed? Do you sigh when you have to pick up your toys? If you talk to God, he will help you do what you need to do. And you may even enjoy it!

My Bible Verse:
God is working in you to help you want to do what pleases him. Then he gives you the power to do it. Philippians 2:13, ICB

My Prayer:
Thank you, God, for your help each day. I want to please you in every way.

Tell Your Friends

4
MARCH

Zoë is talking to a friend. What do you think they are talking about? What kinds of things do you and your friends talk about? It's fun to talk about people and toys and pets. But you can also talk about Jesus. If you love Jesus, God wants you to tell others that he takes care of you and gives you everything you need. Tell your friends—they need to know!

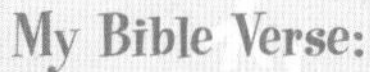

My Bible Verse:

I will tell you what [God] has done for me. Psalm 66:16, ICB

My Prayer:

Help me, Jesus, to tell my friends
About your love that never ends.

5
MARCH

Honor Your Parents

The Bible tells us to honor our parents. That means we need to obey them. We also honor them by being polite. We say please when we ask for something. And we say thank you when they do things for us. How are Kaitlyn and Jack honoring their parents? How can YOU honor your parents? Remember, when you honor your parents, you are also honoring God.

My Bible Verse:
Honor your father and mother. Then you will live a long, full life in the land the Lord your God will give you. Exodus 20:12, NLT

My Prayer:
Help me to honor my parents today
And show them my love as I try to obey.

Good Weapons

Jack is pretending to be a superhero. He is strong and brave because he has some things that will protect him from danger. Do you see his special clothes? Do you see the pan he is using for a shield? What does he have on his head? The Bible tells us about another kind of danger. We have an enemy named Satan. He wants us to disobey God and our parents. But we can protect ourselves from Satan by reading the Bible and praying. Bible reading and prayer will make us strong and keep us safe!

My Bible Verse:

Be strong and brave and wait for the Lord's help. Psalm 27:14, ICB

My Prayer:

Help me, God, to be brave and strong,
To fight against the things that are wrong.

7 MARCH

Have Mercy!

Oh, no! The cat was going to eat Zoë's fish. Bad cat! He hopes Zoë will have mercy on him. That means she will keep on loving him, and she won't stay angry. Do you sometimes do things that are bad? We all do. The bad things are called sins. When we tell God we are sorry for our sins, God has mercy on us and gives us his love. God wants us to have mercy on others just like he has mercy on us.

My Bible Verse:

You are a God of forgiveness, gracious and merciful, slow to become angry, and full of unfailing love and mercy.
Nehemiah 9:17, NLT

My Prayer:

Dear God, your love is easy to see. Thank you for having mercy on me.

Get Excited!

8 MARCH

Jack looks excited, doesn't he? What makes you excited? A new bike? A new friend? A new brother or sister? What else? When we get excited, we feel like shouting or jumping up and down. Do you ever get excited about Jesus? You can jump up and down and tell him you love him. Jesus' love is something very special to get excited about!

My Bible Verse:

O Lord, I will honor and praise your name, for you are my God. You do such wonderful things!
Isaiah 25:1, NLT

My Prayer:

I love you, Jesus, for all that you do. I want to shout my thanks to you.

9

MARCH

Two Are Better

Kaitlyn and Parker are working hard to make pictures for their friends. By working together, they will be able to do more than if they worked alone. There are many times when two people working together are better than one. Making a bed is easier with two. You can build a bigger sand castle with two. And a teeter-totter only works with two! Who can you work with today to get more done?

My Bible Verse:

Two people are better than one. They get more done by working together. Ecclesiastes 4:9, ICB

My Prayer:

Thank you that working together is fun
And a better way to get everything done.

Serve Others

10

MARCH

Zoë is having a tea party. She set a plate of sugar cookies on the table. And she is pouring apple juice from her teapot. But serving friends is more than just giving them food. We also serve others by helping with chores or caring for someone who is sick. Serving others is doing helpful things to show that we love our friends. It also shows that we love God.

My Bible Verse:

Serve one another in love.
Galatians 5:13, NLT

My Prayer:

Lord, I'll show my love for you
And show my love for others, too.

11 MARCH

A Peaceful Feeling

Kaitlyn has a smile on her face because she is feeling peaceful. Do you know what it means to feel peaceful? It means that we are not worried or bothered about anything. When we believe in Jesus, we don't have to worry. He is our friend. He takes care of us. And he helps us with our problems. Doesn't that make you feel peaceful?

My Bible Verse:

[Jesus said,] "I am leaving you with a gift—peace of mind and heart." John 14:27, NLT

My Prayer:

Thank you, Jesus, for the peace that you give.
I want to feel peaceful each day that I live.

Outdoor Fun

Jack, Parker, Zoë, and Kaitlyn like to play outdoors. They went for a walk and decided to visit the cows. Do you like to play outdoors on a nice day? What is your favorite thing to do outside? God made the outdoors for us to enjoy. He could have made the world just for himself, but he didn't. God made the world so he could share it with you.

My Bible Verse:
It is good to be alive to enjoy the light of day.
Ecclesiastes 11:7, ICB

My Prayer:
Thank you for days to play outside
And for the world so big and wide.

13 MARCH

Double Trouble

Uh-oh! Jack and Zoë are having trouble. Zoë was teasing Jack and now he is teasing her. Zoë is afraid of the spider, and Jack thinks that's funny. Do you ever tease a friend? Do you tease your brother or sister? Teasing can be fun if it doesn't hurt the other person. But if teasing is mean and upsets the other person, it can lead to trouble. It's always best to be kind to your friends and family. That way you will not cause trouble.

My Bible Verse:

Even a child is known by his behavior. His actions show if he is innocent and good.
Proverbs 20:11, ICB

My Prayer:

When I'm playing and having fun,
Help me not to hurt anyone.

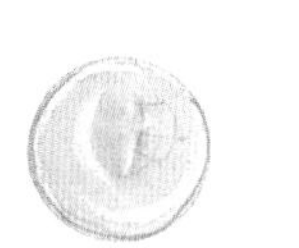

Care for Your Body

14
MARCH

Kaitlyn is soaking in a bubble bath. Do you like taking a bath? Keeping your body clean is a good way to take care of it. You can also care for your body by eating food that's good for you. Can you think of other ways you can take care of your body? God made your body. So it belongs to him. He sends his Holy Spirit to live in each person who loves him. That's why it is important to take good care of the body God has given you.

My Bible Verse:
You should know that your body is a temple for the Holy Spirit. The Holy Spirit is in you. You have received the Holy Spirit from God.
1 Corinthians 6:19, ICB

My Prayer:
Lord, my body belongs to you.
I'll keep it clean and healthy, too.

15 MARCH

Our Helper

Jack is making a big mess. But he isn't getting upset. Jack is being patient and doing his best to clean it up. Whether we are old or young, it is hard to do everything right. That's why God gives us a helper. Do you know who our helper is? Our helper is called the Holy Spirit. The Holy Spirit helps us to be patient and kind. The Holy Spirit helps us know right from wrong. The Holy Spirit fills us with love and joy. Aren't you glad he is your helper?

My Bible Verse:

The Spirit gives love, joy, peace, patience, kindness, goodness, faithfulness, gentleness, self-control.
Galatians 5:22-23, ICB

My Prayer:

Thank you for the Spirit you give
To help me know just how to live.

Fly Away

Can Jack's paper airplanes fly as fast as a bird? No! One minute the bird is right in front of him, and the next minute it's gone! The Bible says that our riches are just like that. One minute we might have lots of money and toys. We're rich! The next minute, we have spent our money, and our toys are broken. Our riches are gone. But God doesn't want us to worry about riches. Being a good person is more important.

My Bible Verse:

Riches can disappear as though they had the wings of a bird!
Proverbs 23:5, NLT

My Prayer:

Money and things will soon be past.
Help me to care about things that will last.

17 MARCH

New Bodies

The children are looking at the rainbow and the pretty clouds. They are thinking about heaven. Someday we will have new bodies that are even more amazing than the bodies we have now. When we go to heaven to live with Jesus, our bodies will be just like his. We won't get sick or hurt. And we'll never have to cry. We will have the best bodies ever!

My Bible Verse:

He will change our simple bodies and make them like his own glorious body. Christ can do this by his power. Philippians 3:21, ICB

My Prayer:

Jesus, when I live with you,
My body will be all brand-new.

Be Happy

18 MARCH

Look at Zoë. She knows that God is helping her to grow up. Can you tell how that makes her feel? God is helping you to grow up too. He will help you when you have problems. He will help you know what he wants you to do. And he will help you to do your best. The more you read the Bible and pray, the more God will help you. That should make you feel happy!

My Bible Verse:
Be glad for all God is planning for you. Be patient in trouble, and always be prayerful.
Romans 12:12, NLT

My Prayer:
Lord, it makes me happy to say
That you will help me all through the day.

19 MARCH

Show It!

Jack isn't saying a word, but he's showing love. How is he doing it? The words "I love you" are very nice words. But it's even more important to show our love than to say the words. You can show your love by being a helper. You can show your love by sharing and being kind. Can you think of other ways to show your love for others? How can you show your love for Jesus?

My Bible Verse:
Dear children, let us stop just saying we love each other; let us really show it by our actions.
1 John 3:18, NLT

My Prayer:
I love you, Jesus. You know it. But today I'll try to show it.

Pray for Others

20 MARCH

Kaitlyn likes to do important things. She knows that one of the most important things she can do is pray. Praying to God is something that boys and girls can do just as well as grown-ups. Have you ever prayed for someone who is sick? Have you ever prayed for someone who is sad? When you pray for other people, God hears your prayers. You can be a big helper by praying for others. Who can you pray for today?

My Bible Verse:
The earnest prayer of a righteous person has great power and wonderful results.
James 5:16, NLT

My Prayer:
Lord, I know you hear my prayer.
Help my friends who need your care.

21
MARCH

Pitter-Patter

Jack and Kaitlyn are trying to stay dry under their big umbrella. Pitter-patter go the raindrops as they come splashing down. Do you know where rain comes from? It comes from the big, gray clouds up in the sky. The rain helps the grass and flowers to grow. The rain makes puddles so tiny birds and furry kittens can get a drink. God knows we need rain. That's why he sends it.

My Bible Verse:

He covers the sky with clouds; he supplies the earth with rain and makes grass grow on the hills. Psalm 147:8, NIV

My Prayer:

Thank you for rain that splashes down
To water the flowers, the trees, and
the ground.

Don't Complain

22
MARCH

Poor Zoë! She can't play on the swings because she hurt her leg. She is sad, but she's not complaining. Parker wants to climb the rope ladder. But Jack says it's his turn. Parker is not complaining. He knows that would spoil a good day. The Bible tells us we should not complain or argue. Can you be like Zoë and Parker? How can you help your friends have a good day?

My Bible Verse:
Do everything without complaining or arguing.
Philippians 2:14, NIV

My Prayer:
Help me, God, to watch what I say
So I will not complain today.

23 MARCH

Help the Weak

Jack was running fast. But he stopped to say hi to a slow-moving turtle. Can you run fast? Can you dress yourself? Can you ride a bike? What else can you do? Not everyone can do the things that you can do. Maybe you have a little brother or sister who is still learning to do many things. God wants you to be patient with little kids and older people who are slower than you. He wants you to wait for them and not get upset with them. He wants you to love them and help them.

My Bible Verse:
Help the weak, be patient with everyone.
1 Thessalonians 5:14, NIV

My Prayer:
Some are weak and some are small.
Lord, I'll try to love them all.

Win or Lose

24
MARCH

"Run, run, run!" yells Jack as loudly as he can. Jack wants his team to win the baseball game. But what if they don't win? Will things be okay? Of course they will. It's always great to win. But losing doesn't take away all the fun. Sometimes losing a game can be good. It makes the team work harder and get better. If we love Jesus, he makes good things happen even when we lose.

My Bible Verse:
We know that in everything God works for the good of those who love him. Romans 8:28, ICB

My Prayer:
In all that happens, help me to see
The good things you have waiting
for me.

25
MARCH

Sing Songs

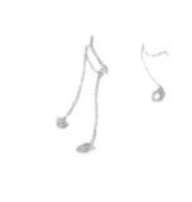

In Bible times, people often said thank you to God by singing songs to him. What are the children in this picture doing? Do you sing songs in church or Sunday school? When we sing songs to God, we show that we love him. We show that we are thankful for all he does for us. Do you know a song you can sing to God? If you don't, you can make up your own!

My Bible Verse:
Then you will sing psalms and hymns and spiritual songs among yourselves, making music to the Lord in your hearts.
Ephesians 5:19, NLT

My Prayer:
Thank you, God, for everything. Listen to the songs I sing.

Take a Look

Who does Zoë see? Who do you see when you look in the mirror? Do you see your eyes? hair? cheeks? teeth? When we look at ourselves and other people, we see what's on the outside. But God cares more about what's on the inside. He looks at our feelings and our thoughts. God sees if we're happy or sad. God sees if we love him and want to obey him. What do you think God sees when he looks inside of you?

My Bible Verse:

God does not see the same way people see. People look at the outside of a person, but the Lord looks at the heart.
1 Samuel 16:7, ICB

My Prayer:

Dear God, when you look at the inside of me,
I want you to like everything that you see.

27 MARCH

Get a Drink

What do you drink when you are thirsty? Zoë is getting a drink of water. It will help her for a little while. But soon she will be thirsty again. That's the way it is with our body. Jesus says that if we believe in him, we will never be thirsty. Jesus is not talking about our body, though. He is talking about our soul. Our soul is inside our body. Our soul needs Jesus just like our body needs water. When we believe in Jesus, our soul won't be thirsty anymore.

My Bible Verse:
He who believes in me will never be thirsty. John 6:35, ICB

My Prayer:
Jesus, your love will fill me up
Like fresh, pure water in my cup.

Life Goes On

28
MARCH

The children are sad because a little bird died. We all feel sad when an animal dies. We're even sadder when people die, because we can't see them anymore. But when people die, only their body dies. The soul inside of them does not die. Jesus tells people to believe in him. Then, after they die, their soul will get a new body and live forever with Jesus in heaven.

My Bible Verse:

[Jesus said,] "I am the resurrection and the life. Those who believe in me, even though they die like everyone else, will live again."
John 11:25, NLT

My Prayer:

Jesus, I know your promise is true. When we die, we will be with you.

29 MARCH

Hard Work

Kaitlyn is working hard today. Folding towels and socks is a big job! Kaitlyn likes to help. She knows her mom and dad are happy when she helps. But the Bible tells us that God is happy when we help too. Do you have work to do today? When you do your work, remember that you are not doing it just for your parents. You are doing it for God, too!

My Bible Verse:

Work with enthusiasm, as though you were working for the Lord rather than for people.
Ephesians 6:7, NLT

My Prayer:

Dear God, when there is work to do, I'll try to do my best for you.

With Jesus

30 MARCH

Zoë's goldfish lives in a bowl of water. It swims up and down and all around. A bowl of water is exactly what Zoë's fish needs to live. The Bible says that people need Jesus to live. When you have Jesus in your heart, he is with you to help you in everything you do. When you get up in the morning, you need Jesus. When you eat your lunch, you need Jesus. When you play outdoors, you need Jesus. Aren't you happy that you're not a goldfish? You don't need a bowl of water. You need Jesus!

My Bible Verse:

For in him we live and move.
Acts 17:28, NLT

My Prayer:

With Jesus I'll eat and work and play.
With Jesus I'll live my life each day.

31 MARCH
Bad Day, Go Away

Jack was having a bad day. He wanted to be alone for a little while. He talked to God and that made him feel better. Now he is happy and wants to play with his friends. Do you ever have a bad day? What makes you feel better? God wants you to talk to him when you are having a bad day. He can make the bad day go away.

My Bible Verse:
If one of you is having troubles, he should pray.
James 5:13, ICB

My Prayer:
When my troubles are getting me down,
You give me a smile instead of a frown.

April

1 APRIL

More Strength

Poor Kaitlyn! She is trying hard to pull the heavy wagon. Kaitlyn wishes she were stronger. Can you think of times when you wished you were stronger? In the Bible, God promises to give us strength. The strength that comes from God is special. It helps us when we are sad. It helps us to obey. And it helps us when we are afraid. God helps us to be strong on the inside.

My Bible Verse:

My sadness has worn me out. Give me strength as you have promised. Psalm 119:28, NIrV

My Prayer:

You make me strong both inside
and out.
Your promises make me want
to shout.

What's in Your Heart?

2
APRIL

Parker wants to know what his heart looks like. Have you ever seen a picture of a heart? The Bible says that God looks at your heart. He doesn't look at it like a doctor does. God looks inside your heart to see if you love him and want to obey him. And do you know what? If you read the Bible and learn what God says, it helps you to do the right things. Then God likes what he sees when he looks at your heart.

My Bible Verse:

I have hidden your word in my heart, that I might not sin against you. Psalm 119:11, NLT

My Prayer:

Lord, I want a loving heart.
Reading your Word is where I'll start.

3 APRIL

Broken Pieces

Why is Zoë sad? Sometimes you might feel so sad that you have a hurt feeling on the inside. When you hurt on the inside, it almost feels like your heart is broken. It can take a long time to feel better. But the good news is that someday you WILL feel better. People who love you will take care of you. God will be close to you. And he will fix the broken feeling in your heart.

My Bible Verse:

The Lord is close to the brokenhearted. He saves those whose spirits have been crushed.

Psalm 34:18, ICB

My Prayer:

Thank you, Lord, that you are close,
Especially when I need you most.

It's a Miracle!

Jack is trying to catch a fish. As he waits, he watches a waterfall splash into the pond. Then he sees a beautiful rainbow. "Wow!" says Jack. "It's a miracle!" Have you ever seen a rainbow? Only God can put a rainbow in the sky. That's why Jack called it a miracle. God can do many marvelous things because no one is as powerful as he is.

My Bible Verse:

You are the God of miracles and wonders! You demonstrate your awesome power among the nations. Psalm 77:14, NLT

My Prayer:

God, I praise you for your power
Every day and every hour.

5

APRIL

The Light of the World

Jack doesn't need light from a lamp to see his book. Do you know why? You're right. The sunlight makes everything bright! Sunlight helps us see so we can work and play. Sunlight helps the trees and flowers grow. Jesus is just like sunlight. He helps us see how we should live. He helps us grow to be better people. We need Jesus just like we need sunlight.

My Bible Verse:

[Jesus said,] "I am the light of the world." John 8:12, NIrV

My Prayer:

Just like the sun, you give us light.
You help us see and learn what's right.

You Can Help

6 APRIL

Kaitlyn and Jack sometimes help their mom and dad by getting them a snack. How can you help your mom and dad? Can you fix a snack? Maybe you can let them rest when they are tired. Can you play quietly with your brother or sister or friend? Can you pick up your toys? These are good things you can do when your mom and dad need your help.

My Bible Verse:
Whenever you are able, do good to people who need help.
Proverbs 3:27, ICB

My Prayer:
When Mom or Dad need a helping hand,
Teach me to do the best that I can.

7

APRIL

Showers of Blessings

Kaitlyn's umbrella is big enough to keep everyone dry. It's just what she needs on a rainy day. Did you know that God will always give you just what you need? The good things that God gives us are called blessings. Your home and family and friends are all blessings. What other good things does God give you? God gives us so many blessings—it's like they come pouring down from heaven!

My Bible Verse:

I will send showers, showers of blessings, which will come just when they are needed.
Ezekiel 34:26, NLT

My Prayer:

Lord, your gifts come pouring down.
Thank you for blessings all around.

Jesus Is Alive

8 APRIL

Kaitlyn and Jack feel sad, because their great-grandma died. But they know she believed in Jesus, God's Son, who died on the cross. Jesus didn't stay dead. He came out of his grave! That's what we celebrate at Easter. It's a special day to remember that Jesus is alive. Now Jesus lives in heaven. Everyone who believes in Jesus will live in heaven someday too.

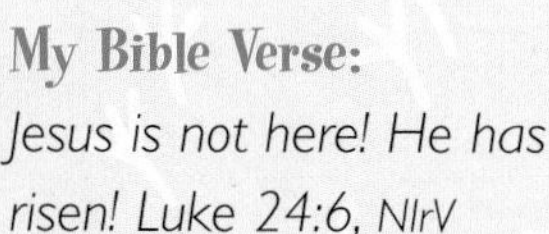

My Bible Verse:
Jesus is not here! He has risen! Luke 24:6, NIrV

My Prayer:
Jesus, you're alive! I know it's true. Someday I'll live in heaven with you!

9 APRIL

God Goes with You

Poor Jack! He doesn't want to go to school today. But do you know what? When he gets to school, he will be happy he is there. Maybe he will paint a pretty picture. Maybe he will listen to a story. And maybe he will play with his friends. Do you ever have times when you don't want to go somewhere? Don't worry about it. God is always with you. And you might even have fun!

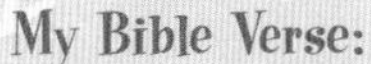

My Bible Verse:

The Lord your God will be with you wherever you go.
Joshua 1:9, NIV

My Prayer:

Lord, it makes me happy to know
That you are with me wherever I go.

Taking Care of Flowers

10
APRIL

Zoë likes to take care of her flowers. She waters the ground and pulls the weeds. The Bible says that God takes care of the flowers too. He sends the sunshine and the rain to help them grow. God cares about the flowers. But he cares about people even more. God loves us more than anything else he made. Does God take good care of the flowers? Then of course he will take care of you!

My Bible Verse:

If God cares so wonderfully for flowers that are here today and gone tomorrow, won't he more surely care for you?
Matthew 6:30, NLT

My Prayer:

Dear God, you care for each flower
and tree,
So I know you'll always take good
care of me.

11 APRIL

Tell the Truth

Do you know why these boys and girls are happy? They always try to tell the truth about each other. They don't make up unkind stories. A story that isn't true is a lie.

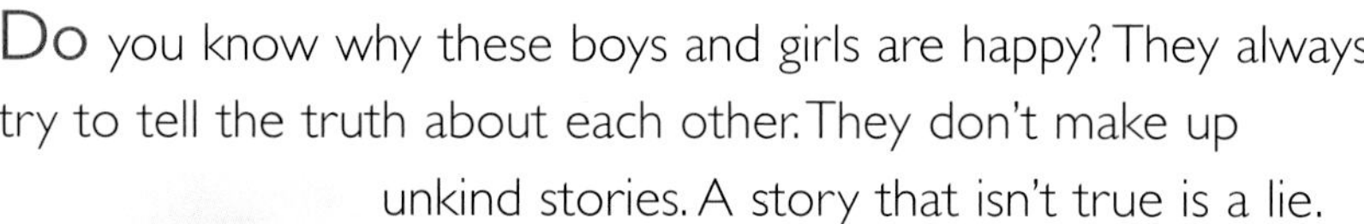

Telling a lie hurts other people. Telling a lie hurts you, too. Telling the truth is always the right thing to do. God wants you to tell the truth to your parents and your friends. Telling the truth makes you feel good inside.

My Bible Verse:
Speak the truth to each other. Zechariah 8:16, NIV

My Prayer:
Help me, Lord, in all that I say
To speak the truth every day.

Thank You, God

12
APRIL

Can you see what Jack is going to do before he eats his cookie? Jack is folding his hands and saying thank you to God. When we pray, we often ask God for things. We ask him to take care of us. We ask him to help our friends. We ask him to keep us safe. Those are all good things to pray about. But it is also important to say thank you to God. We can thank him for everything he gives us each day.

My Bible Verse:
Give thanks to the Lord, for he is good; his love endures forever.
Psalm 107:1, NIV

My Prayer:
Thank you, God, for the good things
you give
To help me enjoy each day that I live.

13

APRIL

Almost like Angels

Kaitlyn is pretending her doll is an angel. God made angels way back at the very beginning. Angels live with God in heaven. They are God's special helpers. Angels are very important. But do you know what? The Bible says that God made you special too! You are more important than anything else on this earth. And someday you will get to live with God and his angels.

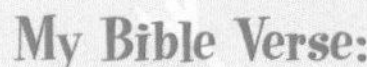

My Bible Verse:

You made man a little lower than the angels. And you crowned him with glory and honor.
Psalm 8:5, ICB

My Prayer:

Lord, I'm important, like angels above.
Help me to give you all of my love.

A Big House

14
APRIL

Jack thinks he can see a big house in the clouds. Do you know why? Jesus lived on the earth a long, long time ago. Then he went to heaven. The Bible says that someday Jesus will come back to earth and take us to heaven to live in his mansion. A mansion is a big house. We can't really see Jesus' big house—not yet. But someday everyone who believes in Jesus will get to live in his mansion with him.

My Bible Verse:
I will come and get you, so that you will always be with me where I am. John 14:3, NLT

My Prayer:
Someday, Lord, I'll go up high
To live in your mansion in the sky.

15

APRIL

Think about Good Things

Parker likes to sneak up into a tree. He can sit there and think about good things, like trees and birds and the big sky God made. He doesn't think about bad things, like being angry or unkind. The Bible tells us to think only about good things. We can think about people we love and things that make us happy. What are some good things you like to think about?

My Bible Verse:

Continue to think about the things that are good and worthy of praise.
Philippians 4:8, ICB

My Prayer:

Dear Lord Jesus, help my mind
To think about things that are good and kind.

Be Ready!

16
APRIL

Can you guess who is inside the yellow raincoat? It's Jack! He is ready to go fishing. Do you think he has everything he needs? It's good to be ready for the things we do. When we go on a picnic, we get snacks ready. When we play in the snow, we put on boots and mittens. The Bible tells us to be ready to serve. That means we need to learn how to help others. And we need to be ready to do many good things. If we are ready to serve, then we will be ready when Jesus comes back too!

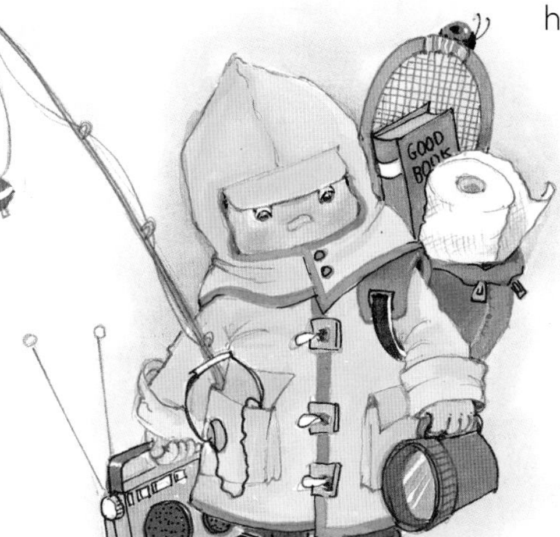

My Bible Verse:

Be dressed and ready to serve.
Luke 12:35, NIrV

My Prayer:

Lord, teach me the things I need to know
To be ready to help wherever I go.

17 APRIL

Three Times a Day

How many times do you think Jack prays each day? The Bible tells the story of a man named Daniel who prayed three times every day. The king made a bad rule that said everyone had to pray to him. Daniel knew it was wrong to pray to the king. He kept praying to God. Daniel was thrown into a lions' den for doing that. But God kept Daniel safe. The king let Daniel out of the lions' den and changed his bad rule.

My Bible Verse:

[Daniel] went to his room three times a day to pray. He got down on his knees and gave thanks to his God. Daniel 6:10, NIrV

My Prayer:

Lord, I know you want me to pray
Many times all through the day.

Best Friends

18
APRIL

Kaitlyn and Zoë are measuring themselves. They are best friends. Sometimes they make pictures together. And sometimes they just talk and laugh. There are many things that friends can do together. What do you like to do with your friends? Whatever you do, God wants you to love them and be kind to them. He wants you to care about them. What can you do to be kind to your friends?

My Bible Verse:
Do what is right to other people. Love being kind to others.
Micah 6:8, ICB

My Prayer:
Dear God, my friends are special to me.
Loving and kind is the way I should be.

19

APRIL

Tell about Jesus

Everyone likes to listen when Kaitlyn tells stories. The Bible tells us many stories about Jesus. Jesus made storms go away. Jesus fed thousands of hungry people with only a little bit of food. Jesus healed people who were sick. He even made blind people able to see. Do you know other stories about Jesus? Don't keep them to yourself. Tell them to your friends!

My Bible Verse:
Never be ashamed to tell others about our Lord.
2 Timothy 1:8, NLT

My Prayer:
Jesus, the stories about you are great.
Please help me to share them—
I just can't wait!

Looking for Water

20
APRIL

Shhh! Kaitlyn and Zoë are being very quiet. They see a deer looking for water. Have you ever seen a deer? A deer needs water to drink, just like we do. The deer looks for water until he finds it. Just like a deer looks for water, we can look for God. We can see God's beauty in a sunset. We can read God's words in the Bible. We can talk to God in prayer. When we look for God, we always find him.

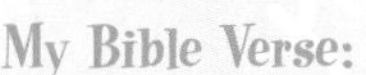

My Bible Verse:

A deer longs for streams of water. God, I long for you in the same way. Psalm 42:1, NIrV

My Prayer:

Dear God, I want to find out where you are.
I know I won't have to look very far!

21 APRIL

Run Home

Uh-oh! Kaitlyn and her friends were playing outdoors and now it's raining. They're running home so they won't get wet. Do you run home when it rains? Do you run home when you get hurt or when you feel afraid? It's good to run home when you have a problem. God wants you to run to HIM when you need help too. He wants to take care of you. But you don't need to use your legs to run to God. All you need to do is close your eyes and pray!

My Bible Verse:

Feel free to come before God's throne. Here there is grace. And we can receive mercy and grace to help us when we need it.
Hebrews 4:16, ICB

My Prayer:

Dear God, I know you're always there,
Waiting to help me because you care.

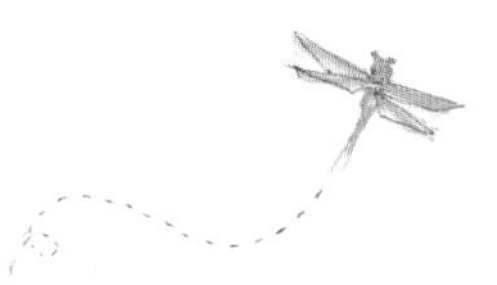

Satisfied

22 APRIL

Do you know what the word *satisfied* means? It means that you are happy with what you have. Zoë feels satisfied because she has a full stomach and a big, soft dog for a pillow! Sometimes we think we need more candy, more toys, more clothes, or more money. But Jesus is the only one who can help us be satisfied. When we love Jesus, he gives us everything we need.

My Bible Verse:

You open your hand and satisfy the needs of every living creature.
Psalm 145:16, NIrV

My Prayer:

Jesus, all I need is you.
You satisfy me through and through.

23
APRIL

God Watches You

Kaitlyn is watching some animal friends as she helps them cross a path. Did you know that God watches you wherever you go? He helps to keep you safe. Do you ever go to your neighbor's house? Do you ever go to the playground? Where else do you go? If you are with your friends or if you are alone, God is always watching you. Even when you are sleeping, God watches over you to keep you safe.

My Bible Verse:
The Lord sees everything you do. He watches where you go.
Proverbs 5:21, ICB

My Prayer:
Whether I go here or there,
Lord, you watch me everywhere.

God's House

24 APRIL

Kaitlyn and Jack are looking at a beautiful window in their church. Do you ever go to church? A church is where people who love God come to sing and worship. They come to read the Bible and learn more about God. Even though God is always with you at your house, he wants you to come to his house too. The people who come to God's house are part of God's family. It is very special to come together at God's house.

My Bible Verse:

I was glad when they said to me, "Let us go to the house of the Lord." Psalm 122:1, NLT

My Prayer:

Dear God, it's a very special day
Whenever I go to your house to
pray.

25 APRIL
A New Person

Zoë is giving her dolls a haircut. That may not be a good idea! But sometimes it's okay to change the way we look. We may get a haircut or wear new clothes. It's almost like we become a new person on the outside. When you tell Jesus you love him, you become a new person on the inside. You are filled with Jesus' love. You want to please God instead of yourself. Jesus changes you into the person that God wants you to be.

My Bible Verse:
Those who become Christians become new persons. They are not the same anymore.
2 Corinthians 5:17, NLT

My Prayer:
Jesus, I want to be brand-new
And live my life to honor you.

Hold On!

26
APRIL

Kaitlyn and Jack are zooming down the hill in their wagon. They'd better hold on tight so they won't fall out! Holding on to things keeps us safe. We hold on to railings when we go down the stairs. We hold each other's hands to cross the street. Can you think of other times when you need to hold on? The Bible tells us to hold on to God and what he teaches. That means we should read Bible stories and learn to obey him.

My Bible Verse:
Love the Lord your God, listen to his voice, and hold fast to him.
Deuteronomy 30:20, NIV

My Prayer:
Lord, I'll try to do what is right.
I'll listen to you and hold on tight.

27 APRIL

Making Plans

Kaitlyn thinks she wants to be a teacher someday. Jack wants to play football when he grows up. What do you think Zoë and Parker want to do? What do you want to do someday? You may not know the answer yet, but you can talk to God about it. He will help you study and learn. He will help you know what to do. If you ask for God's help, things will work out the way he wants them to.

My Bible Verse:

Depend on the Lord in whatever you do. Then your plans will succeed. Proverbs 16:3, ICB

My Prayer:

I'm not sure what I'm going to be,
But I know you'll be right there with me.

Always the Same

28
APRIL

Look at the sun in the sky. Have you noticed that the sun comes up every morning? Have you noticed that it gets dark every night? Did you know that spring always comes after winter, and fall always comes after summer? God made the sun and the seasons to always do the same things. So we can count on God to always do the same things too. God never changes. He will always love you, and he will always be with you.

My Bible Verse:
I am the Lord, and I do not change. Malachi 3:6, NLT

My Prayer:
God, you're the same day after day. I'm glad it will always be that way.

29 APRIL

Don't Hide It!

Parker is looking for his friends. Can you help him? It's fun to play hiding games. We can hide toys or treats or even ourselves! But there is one thing we must never hide—and that is our love for Jesus. If you love Jesus, you won't want to hide that from anyone. Tell your friends everything you know about Jesus, so they can know him too.

My Bible Verse:

I am proud of the Good News. It is the power God uses to save everyone who believes.
Romans 1:16, ICB

My Prayer:

Jesus, your love is too good to hide. Help me not to keep it inside.

Thank You for Friends

30

APRIL

Jack is waving good-bye to his friends. They had fun playing together. Even though they are going home, Jack can still be happy about his friends. He can pray for them and thank God for them. Do you have friends that you like to play with? Even when you are not with them, remember to pray for them. Say thank you to God for your friends.

My Bible Verse:

I thank my God every time
I remember you.
Philippians 1:3, NIV

My Prayer:

God, I thank you for my friends
Even when our playtime ends.

May

God Is Very Great

1
MAY

Jack is looking out his window. He sees the trees and the grass. He sees the beautiful sky God made. What does Jack see in the sky? God is very great and powerful. Only God can make trees and rainbows. Can you think of other things God made? When we look at everything God created, it helps us understand how great and awesome he is.

My Bible Verse:

You are great. You do wonderful things. You alone are God.
Psalm 86:10, NIrV

My Prayer:

I look outside and then I see
Your awesome greatness all around me.

2

MAY

Good Medicine

Poor Jack! His friends are playing outdoors. But he is sick in bed. He even has to take medicine! Have you ever had to stay in bed when you were sick? Have you ever had to take medicine? Being sick is not much fun. But taking medicine helps you feel better. The Bible says that being happy is like taking good medicine. Being happy helps you feel better. And it doesn't even taste bad!

My Bible Verse:

A happy heart is like good medicine. Proverbs 17:22, ICB

My Prayer:

Whenever I'm sick and feeling sad,
Help me to soon feel well and glad.

Tasty Treats

3

MAY

Yum, yum! Jack is waiting for Kaitlyn to give him his ice cream treat. What is your favorite kind of ice cream? Ice cream tastes good—especially on a sunny day! God wants us to enjoy him just like we enjoy tasty treats. You can enjoy God by listening to your favorite Bible story. You can enjoy God by saying your favorite prayer. And you can enjoy God by singing your favorite song.

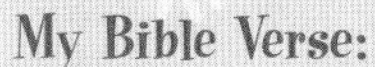

My Bible Verse:
Taste and see that the Lord is good. Oh, the joys of those who trust in him! Psalm 34:8, NLT

My Prayer:
I want to enjoy you every day
And trust in you as I sing and pray.

4

MAY

A Special Friend

Kaitlyn is Zoë's special friend, and Zoë is Kaitlyn's special friend. They like being together. Do you have a special friend you like to be with? Maybe you have a brother or sister for a friend. Did you know that Jesus wants to be your friend too? If you love Jesus and obey him, he will be your special friend. You can talk to him anytime. You can even talk to him at night when your other friends are at home in their own bed. Jesus is the best friend you will ever have.

My Bible Verse:

You are my friends if you obey me. John 15:14, NLT

My Prayer:

Jesus, I'm glad you want to be
A very special friend to me.

Playing Tricks

5
MAY

Uh-oh! Jack and Parker are playing a trick on Kaitlyn. Do you think she will get upset? Do you like to play tricks on your friends? It's fun to play tricks as long as you're not being mean. God sees everything that you do. He sees when you obey. And he sees when you disobey. God watches when you play tricks on your friends. He doesn't want your tricks to be mean.

My Bible Verse:
The eyes of the Lord are everywhere, keeping watch on the wicked and the good.
Proverbs 15:3, NIV

My Prayer:
Lord, you watch me when I play.
Help me to be good today.

6

MAY

The Good Shepherd

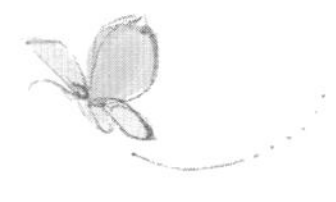

Do you go to your mom when she calls? You know the sound of her voice, don't you? When a shepherd like Parker calls his sheep, they go to him because they know his voice. The sheep know that the shepherd loves them and takes care of them. The Bible says that Jesus is our Good Shepherd. Jesus loves us and cares for us. You can learn to know your Shepherd by reading stories about Jesus in the Bible.

My Bible Verse:

I am the good shepherd; I know my own sheep, and they know me.
John 10:14, NLT

My Prayer:

Dear Lord Jesus, it's my choice
To follow you and know your voice.

One Big Family

7 MAY

Jack, Zoë, Kaitlyn, and Parker play together and help each other. They are almost like one big family. Did you know that you are part of a very big family? You have a family that you live with every day. But if you love Jesus, you are also part of God's big family. God wants the people in his family to love each other and help each other, just like brothers and sisters.

My Bible Verse:

Live together in peace. Be understanding. Love one another like members of the same family.
1 Peter 3:8, NIrV

My Prayer:

Help me to love my sisters and brothers
By being kind and helping others.

8
MAY

A Crown for You

Have you ever seen a crown on someone's head? It can be made of silver or gold. It can be made of diamonds or even flowers, like the one Kaitlyn is putting on Jack's head. When a person wears a crown, it means he is important. You are important to God. That's why he gives you a crown of blessings. This crown isn't really for your head, though! God gives you a family and friends. He gives you a place to live and food to eat. Each of these blessings from God is like a crown.

My Bible Verse:
Blessings are like crowns on the heads of those who do right.
Proverbs 10:6, NIrV

My Prayer:
Thank you for blessings I wear like
a crown
And all of the love that you keep
sending down.

Hope in the Lord

9

MAY

Zoë feels bad because her grandpa is in the hospital. But she has hope that God will take care of him. That hope makes her happy enough to blow bubbles! Do you know what it means to have hope? It means that when things are really bad, you believe they will get better. When you love God, you can always have hope. No matter how bad something is, God will help you get through it. With God as your heavenly Father, there are always better days ahead.

My Bible Verse:

Be strong, all of you who put your hope in the Lord.
Psalm 31:24, NIrV

My Prayer:

Lord, when bad things come my way,
I know I'll soon have a better day.

10
MAY

More than Enough

Parker and his friends are having a picnic. They have more food than they can eat. So they are sharing their food with their animal friends. Sometimes God gives us more than we need. Do you ever have extra food to share? Can you share your toys or clothes with someone? We can use our extra things to help others.

My Bible Verse:

God will generously provide all you need. Then you will always have everything you need and plenty left over to share with others. 2 Corinthians 9:8, NLT

My Prayer:

Lord, when you give me more than
I need,
Help me to share and do a good
deed.

One of a Kind

Kaitlyn is using chalk to draw around Zoë on a big piece of paper. Do you know how you look? How tall are you? What color is your hair? Do you have freckles? Guess what? There is no one else exactly like you! God made you just the way he wanted you to be. Your eyes, your skin, even your laugh are your very own. God made everything on your outside and everything on your inside. That should make you feel very special!

My Bible Verse:
You made me and formed me with your own hands.
Psalm 119:73, NIrV

My Prayer:
Dear Lord, you made me as I am,
According to your perfect plan.

12 MAY

God's Glory

Jack is almost ready for bed. He is looking out the window just in time to see a beautiful sunset. What colors does he see? Have you ever seen a sunset? God is the one who puts all the pretty colors in the sky. When we see a sunset, it shows us God's glory. Glory is another word for greatness. Only God is great enough and powerful enough to make a beautiful sunset.

My Bible Verse:

The skies tell about his goodness.
And all the people see his glory.
Psalm 97:6, ICB

My Prayer:

You're my God in heaven on high.
Dear Lord, your greatness fills the sky.

Healthy Trees

13
MAY

Zoë is watering a plant. Have you ever done that? Some plants grow into big trees. They need water to grow big and stay healthy. Some trees grow fruit like oranges and apples. Just like trees need water, we need the Bible. Reading the Bible helps us grow to be like Jesus. It helps us understand how God wants us to live. When we love and obey God, we are like a healthy tree that grows a lot of fruit.

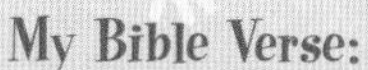

My Bible Verse:

He is like a tree planted by streams of water, which yields its fruit in season.
Psalm 1:3, NIV

My Prayer:

Lord, teach me all I need to know
So I can please you as I grow.

14 MAY

The Holy Spirit

Zoë is happy because she knows she is not alone. When Jesus went to heaven, he told his friends not to be sad. He said he was sending them a helper. His helper is the Holy Spirit. Zoë cannot see the Holy Spirit. We can't either, but he lives in us when we believe in Jesus. The Holy Spirit helps us obey. The Holy Spirit comforts us when we are sad. The Holy Spirit helps us understand the words in the Bible. The Holy Spirit helps us know that God loves us.

My Bible Verse:
The Spirit is God's guarantee that he will give us everything he promised. Ephesians 1:14, NLT

My Prayer:
May your Holy Spirit guide me.
I'm glad he'll always stay inside me.

Be Happy Anyway

15
MAY

Poor Kaitlyn broke her leg! She won't be able to run around and play for a while. So why do you think she is smiling? Maybe she is happy just to be outdoors. She can watch the butterflies and talk to her animal friends. Kaitlyn knows that after a while her leg will be better. Even when something bad happens, we can still find things to be happy about. And we can please God by trusting him.

My Bible Verse:

You will have many kinds of troubles. But when these things happen, you should be very happy. You know that these things are testing your faith. And this will give you patience.
James 1:2-3, ICB

My Prayer:

Help me, God, to be happy today
Even if troubles come my way.

16 MAY

Getting Close

Kaitlyn and her little brother, Jack, are snuggling in a big chair. Who do you like to snuggle with? It feels good to be near someone you love. Did you know that you can be near God, too? You can come near to God by reading about him in the Bible. You can come near to God by praying. You can come near to God by looking at the trees and the flowers he made. And when you come near to God, he will come near to you!

My Bible Verse:

Come near to God and he will come near to you. James 4:8, NIV

My Prayer:

Dear God, I know you're always right here
Whenever I need you and want to be near.

Every Day

17 MAY

Zoë brushes her teeth every morning and every night. When do you brush your teeth? Do you get dressed every morning? When do you eat breakfast and lunch and dinner? What other things do you do every day? It's good to do all those things. But there is something else that's good to do every day. It's good to talk about God's love. God loves you so much, you should talk about it every day. You should talk about it the first thing every morning and the last thing each night!

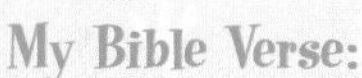

My Bible Verse:

It is good to tell of your love in the morning and of your loyalty at night. Psalm 92:2, ICB

My Prayer:

Lord, you love me—there's no doubt.
It's something I'll always talk about.

18
MAY

Growing Up

Zoë is happy that she is growing up. She is learning to comb her hair and to do many other things, just like you are. Are you learning to count and to dress yourself? Are you learning to be a helper? Are you learning to obey your parents? These are things that God is helping you learn. God will help you learn many more good things as you keep growing. What are some things you want God to help you learn?

My Bible Verse:

God began doing a good work in you. And he will continue it until it is finished.
Philippians 1:6, ICB

My Prayer:

Thank you, Lord, that you're helping me
To be the person you want me to be.

Taking Care of the World

19
MAY

A long, long time ago God made the world and everything in it. In this picture, can you see some things God made? Ever since the beginning of the world, God has been taking care of it. He takes care of the animals and helps them find food. He sends rain when the grass and the trees and the flowers get thirsty. He makes the sun shine to keep us warm and give us light. Can you think of other ways that God is taking care of the world he made?

Yes, God made all things. And everything continues through God and for God.
Romans 11:36, ICB

My Prayer:

Oh, God, you care for everything—
From trees and flowers, to birds that sing!

20 MAY

Don't Doubt It

Do you know what it means to doubt? It means that you're not sure if something is true or not. You go back and forth, just like the waves in the sea go up and down. But with God, we never have to doubt anything. God cannot lie. So we can believe everything that he says in the Bible. People who doubt God get mixed up. Don't doubt what God says—believe it!

My Bible Verse:
Do not doubt God. Anyone who doubts is like a wave in the sea. The wind blows the wave up and down. James 1:6, ICB

My Prayer:
Dear Lord, I will never doubt you,
For every word you say is true.

Be a Good Example

21
MAY

Parker is giving his friends a ride in his wagon. He enjoys being kind to his friends and making them happy. Parker is being a good example. You can be a good example too. You can wait for your turn in line. You can let your friends play with your toys. You can say please and thank you. What other ways can you be a good example?

My Bible Verse:
You yourself must be an example . . . by doing good deeds of every kind.
Titus 2:7, NLT

My Prayer:
Help me to be an example today
By the things I do and the words I say.

22 MAY

Respect God

Do you think Zoë looks content? Maybe it's because she respects God. Do you know what it means to respect God? It means that you show your love for God by obeying him. When you love and obey God, he will take care of you. Then you don't need to worry about anything. When you respect God, problems won't bother you because you know that God will take care of things. When you respect God, you can rest, just like Zoë.

My Bible Verse:

Having respect for the Lord leads to life. Then you will be content and free from trouble.

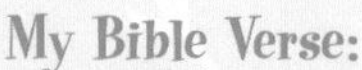
Proverbs 19:23, NIrV

My Prayer:

Respecting you, Lord, is always best.
Instead of worrying, I can rest.

God Can Do More

23
MAY

These children can do many things without a grown-up. What can you do without help? Can you put on your socks? Can you brush your teeth? You can do many things by yourself. But when a grown-up helps, you can do more things, like bake a cake or build a fort. What else can you do? God is so big and powerful, he can help you do even more than you and a grown-up can do together!

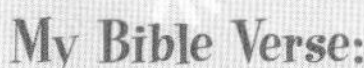

My Bible Verse:

With God's power working in us, God can do much, much more than anything we can ask or think of.
Ephesians 3:20, ICB

My Prayer:

Jesus, you can help me do more
Than anything I have done before.

24 MAY

Good Morning, God

Kaitlyn and her friends are just waking up. "Good morning, God!" says Kaitlyn. She doesn't see God, but she sees the beautiful morning sun he created. Did you see the sun this morning? Can you see the big, blue sky? Do you see the stars at night? We can see God all around us by looking at the things he made.

My Bible Verse:

He calls out to the earth from the sunrise in the east to the sunset in the west. Psalm 50:1, NIrV

My Prayer:

If I look up or if I look down,
God, I can see you all around.

Build It Up!

25
MAY

Parker and Zoë are helping Jack build a tall tower. "Come on, Jack!" says Zoë. "You can do it!" When friends help and encourage one another, they can do things much better. Do you like it when people help you and cheer you on? When we encourage others, we build them up. We help them believe that they can do lots of things. Can you build up your sister or brother or friend today? Come on! You can do it!

My Bible Verse:
So encourage each other and build each other up, just as you are already doing.
1 Thessalonians 5:11, NLT

My Prayer:
Building up others is what I will do
To help my friends and, Lord, to
please you.

26 MAY

Coming and Going

Jack and his friends are running all over the place. Sometimes they play on the swings, and sometimes they just run around. Sometimes they play outdoors, and sometimes they play in the house. Do you go lots of different places? Do you go to the store or to your grandma's house? The Bible says that God watches over you everywhere you go.

My Bible Verse:

The Lord will watch over your coming and going both now and forevermore. Psalm 121:8, NIV

My Prayer:

*Whenever I come and whenever I go,
Lord, you are with me, this I know.*

Bedtime Tears

27
MAY

It's time for bed and Zoë is crying. Her favorite bunny has a hole—right in the middle of his tummy! "Don't cry, Zoë! Your mommy can fix your bunny, and everything will be all right." Zoë will feel better after a good night's sleep. Do you ever feel like crying at bedtime? When you are tired, things seem worse than they really are. The Bible says that you might feel sad for a while, but God can help you feel happy again.

My Bible Verse:

Crying may last for a night.
But joy comes in the morning.
Psalm 30:5, ICB

My Prayer:

Dear God, when I've been sad at night,
I wake up glad in the morning light.

28

MAY

What Time Is It?

Do you have a watch like Jack has? Look at the sundial. The shadow from the sun points to the right time, just like a clock does. Clocks help us know what time it is. In the morning, it's time to get up. At noon, it's time for lunch. God created the world so that there is a special time for the things we need to do each day. Do you play in the middle of the night? Of course not! There are times to play and times to rest. What time is it right now?

My Bible Verse:

There is a right time for everything. Everything on earth has its special season. Ecclesiastes 3:1, ICB

My Prayer:

Thank you for times when I can have fun,
And for times to rest when each day is done.

Start with Prayer

Jack just got dressed. He hasn't had breakfast yet. What's he doing? Yes, he's praying! Jack likes to talk to God the first thing every morning. Can you do that too? You can thank God for a brand-new day. You can ask him to keep you safe. You can ask him to help you obey. You can even ask God to give your mom and dad a good day. Starting with prayer is the best way to start your day!

My Bible Verse:

Lord, every morning you hear my voice. Every morning, I tell you what I need.
Psalm 5:3, ICB

My Prayer:

Dear God, in the morning you hear my prayer,
And all through the day I am in your care.

30

MAY

God Made Everything

Jack is thinking about how great and mighty God is. God created the giant mountains and the oceans that are very deep and very wide. He put the sun and clouds in the sky. He put the birds in the air and the fish in the sea. Everything God made shows us how great he is. Everything God made is wonderful. But the most wonderful thing God made is you! And you can praise God for being so great.

My Bible Verse:

Praise the Lord, everything he has created, everywhere in his kingdom. As for me—I, too, will praise the Lord. Psalm 103:22, NLT

My Prayer:

Lord, I want to give you praise
For all your great and mighty ways.

All I Need

Kaitlyn has everything she needs. She has snacks to munch on. She has friends to play with. And she has a big umbrella to shade her from the sun. There are many things that we need each day. We need food to eat and water to drink. We need clothes to wear and a place to live. But we don't have to worry about these things. In the Bible, God promises to give us everything we need.

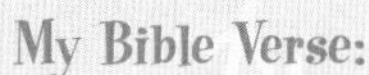

My Bible Verse:

My God will use his wonderful riches in Christ Jesus to give you everything you need.
Philippians 4:19, ICB

My Prayer:

My house, my food, my clothing too—
All these blessings come from you.

June

Look Straight Ahead

1 JUNE

Jack kicks his football in the air. "Go fetch it!" says Jack to his dog. Have you ever tried to kick a football? It's important to look straight ahead and keep your eyes on the ball. If you don't, you might miss the ball when you try to kick it. The Bible tells us to look straight ahead and keep our eyes on things that are right and good. Then we'll be safe. And we won't miss all the great things that God has for us.

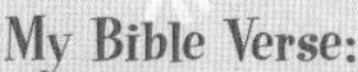

My Bible Verse:

Keep your eyes focused on what is right. Keep looking straight ahead to what is good. Proverbs 4:25, ICB

My Prayer:

Help me to look at the things that
I should—
Things that are right and things
that are good.

2

JUNE

Be Careful What You Say

Do you like to play with your friends? It's fun to laugh and talk while you play. But it's important to say things that are kind. It's important to say things that are helpful. And it's important to say things that are true. What do you think the kids in this picture are saying? When you are careful about what you say, you won't cause trouble.

My Bible Verse:

A person who is careful about what he says keeps himself out of trouble. Proverbs 21:23, ICB

My Prayer:

Help me, Jesus, whenever I play
To be careful with all of the words I say.

A New Day

3
JUNE

Zoë is getting her own breakfast today. Oops! She spilled a little milk on the table—but she can wipe it up. And tomorrow will be a brand-new day. If you have a bad day today, you can start all over again tomorrow. That's how it is with God too. If you do something that's wrong, you can tell God you are sorry. God will forgive you. He will keep on loving you. And he will give you a brand-new day to start all over again.

My Bible Verse:
His great love is new every morning. Lord, how faithful you are! Lamentations 3:23, NIrV

My Prayer:
Thank you that every day is new. Help me, dear God, to live for you.

4

JUNE

The Good Earth

Jack and Parker are enjoying a big juicy watermelon on a warm summer day. In the summer we have lots of fresh fruit to eat. Do you like watermelon and strawberries? How about peaches and blueberries? All these good things come from God. The earth is full of yummy things that God made for us to enjoy.

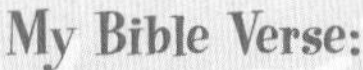

My Bible Verse:

Lord, you have made many things. With your wisdom you made them all. The earth is full of your riches.
Psalm 104:24, ICB

My Prayer:

Thank you, Lord, for good things to eat
That fill my tummy and taste so sweet.

Rejoice Always

5 JUNE

Why do you think Zoë is so happy? Maybe it's because she loves Jesus and she knows that Jesus loves her! Do you know what it means to rejoice? It means to be really happy. You might be really happy when it's a special day like your birthday or Christmas. You might be really happy when a friend comes over to play. But if you love Jesus, then you have a reason to be really happy every day.

My Bible Verse:

Rejoice in the Lord always. I will say it again: Rejoice!
Philippians 4:4, NIV

My Prayer:

Every day and every season
I will rejoice, for you are the reason.

6
JUNE

Time to Celebrate

Today is Jack's birthday! Do you like parties? It's fun to celebrate birthdays and special holidays with our family and friends. But did you know that we have something to celebrate every day of the year? The Bible says that God is good. So be happy and celebrate! You don't have to wait until it's your birthday. You can have a party today and celebrate the goodness of God.

My Bible Verse:
They will celebrate your great goodness. They will sing with joy about your holy acts.
Psalm 145:7, NIrV

My Prayer:
Dear God, you are so good and great, I want to sing and celebrate!

Jesus Loves Children

Did you know that Jesus loves children very much? One day many grown-ups and children were trying to get close to Jesus. His helpers tried to keep the children away. They thought the children would bother Jesus. But Jesus said he wanted the children to come to him. Jesus said that children are a special part of God's family. He loves boys and girls like the ones in the picture. And he loves *you*!

My Bible Verse:

Let the children come to me. Don't stop them! For the Kingdom of God belongs to such as these.
Mark 10:14, NLT

My Prayer:

Jesus, I'm glad you want me to be
A special part of God's family.

8
JUNE

Sweet Words

Jack is pouring sweet honey on his pancakes. Do you like to put honey or syrup on your pancakes? Most boys and girls enjoy food that tastes sweet. The Bible says that God's words are so special, they are sweeter than honey. We can enjoy God's words by reading them in the Bible. God's words are sweet like honey because they are good and they help us to be happy. God's words are the best thing in the whole world!

My Bible Verse:

How sweet are your words to my taste; they are sweeter than honey.
Psalm 119:103, NLT

My Prayer:

Thank you, Lord, for food to eat
And for your words so kind and sweet.

Waiting for Good Things

9
JUNE

Kaitlyn is so excited! She and her family are going to a camp where they will have lots of fun. She waited and waited. And now the special day is here. Have you ever had to wait for something special? It's hard to wait for something that we know is going to be very good. The Bible says that God has many good things for us on earth. But he also will have good things for us in heaven someday. Everything that God has for us is worth waiting for.

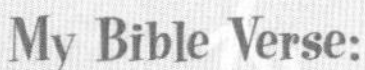

My Bible Verse:

I wait for the Lord, my soul waits, and in his word I put my hope. Psalm 130:5, NIV

My Prayer:

Lord, it's sometimes hard to wait,
But what you give is very great.

10 JUNE

Live at Peace

Are the kids in this picture fighting? No! They are happy as they peacefully walk along together. Do you ever fight with a friend or with someone in your family? God doesn't want us to fight. He wants us to live in peace with the people around us. Sometimes it's hard to be at peace with everyone. But if you love Jesus, he can help you to get along and not fight with your friends and family.

My Bible Verse:

Try your best to live in peace with everyone.
Hebrews 12:14, NIrV

My Prayer:

Dear God, I know that peace is good
In my home and neighborhood.

The Right Thing to Do

11
JUNE

The children are coming out of their rooms to play. They will have fun if they obey God's rules. That's because God knows the right things to do. God tells us to be kind and to share and not to fight. When you do what God tells you to do, you're doing the right thing. It's hard to do what's right all the time. But when you disobey, you can tell God you are sorry. Then God will forgive you.

My Bible Verse:

The right thing for us to do is this: Obey all these rules in the presence of the Lord our God. Deuteronomy 6:25, ICB

My Prayer:

Help me, Lord, to do what is right
With all of my strength and all of
my might.

12 JUNE

Care about Others

Kaitlyn is almost ready for bed. She put on her favorite pajamas and found her favorite doll. But Kaitlyn is checking to make sure that her cat is okay too. Do you have a pet that you check on? Do you ever see if your mom is okay? Do you have a brother or sister that you care about? We need to take care of ourselves. But it's important to care about others, too.

My Bible Verse:

Do not be interested only in your own life, but be interested in the lives of others.
Philippians 2:4, ICB

My Prayer:

Lord, help me to care about others too. I know that's what you want me to do.

A Rainbow of Colors

Jack is painting a pretty picture. He is using lots of colors. Did you know that when God created the world, he also created lots of colors? He made a yellow sun. He made a blue sky. And he made green grass. Can you think of other colors that God made? These colors show how great God is—they show his glory. Every time you look outside, you can see God's beautiful colors. And you know how great he is!

My Bible Verse:
May the whole earth be filled with his glory. Psalm 72:19, NIV

My Prayer:
Thank you, God, for colors so bright
That make the world a beautiful sight.

14 JUNE

Enjoy It

Kaitlyn loves to walk on the beach and find seashells. She enjoys the sound of the splashing waves. And she likes to feel the sand on her bare feet. What are some things that you like to do? God is happy when we can do the things we enjoy. One of the things God wants us to enjoy is obeying him. Do you want to obey God? Bible stories and Bible verses help you know what God wants you to do. Be sure to learn all you can so you'll enjoy obeying God.

My Bible Verse:
I take joy in doing your will, my God. Psalm 40:8, NLT

My Prayer:
My heart is happy when I obey. I want to enjoy you every day.

You Are a Miracle!

15
JUNE

Kaitlyn is holding a baby boy on her lap. Have you ever held a baby? Babies are a special gift from God. You were once a baby too. But before you were even born, God created you inside your mommy's tummy. God made your eyes and your nose and your fingers and your toes. Can you count your fingers and your toes? Can you look in a mirror to see how special you are? You are a miracle!

My Bible Verse:

You made my whole being. You formed me in my mother's body.
Psalm 139:13, ICB

My Prayer:

Lord, I'm a miracle! Yes, it's true.
Every part of my body was made by you.

16 JUNE

Trust in God

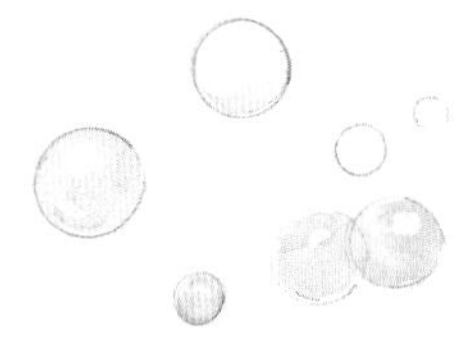

Do you know what it means to trust? It means to believe everything will be okay. We trust that our parents will take care of us. We trust that our beds will keep us warm. We trust that God will always love us and protect us.

What is Jack trusting God to do? The Bible tells us that we can be happy when we trust in God. When you trust in God, he shows you what to do. And you don't have to worry about anything.

My Bible Verse:
May the God of hope fill you with all joy and peace as you trust in him. Romans 15:13, NIV

My Prayer:
Help me, Lord, to trust you today
To keep me safe as I work and play.

Help When You're Hurt

17
JUNE

Uh-oh! Parker fell down and scraped his knee. Zoë and Kaitlyn are helping him so he will feel better. Who helps you when you get hurt? Does your mom or dad or grandma help you? The Bible says that God's Holy Spirit will help you also. Whether you are feeling bad on the inside or hurting on the outside, just pray to God. His Holy Spirit is always right there with you to help you feel better.

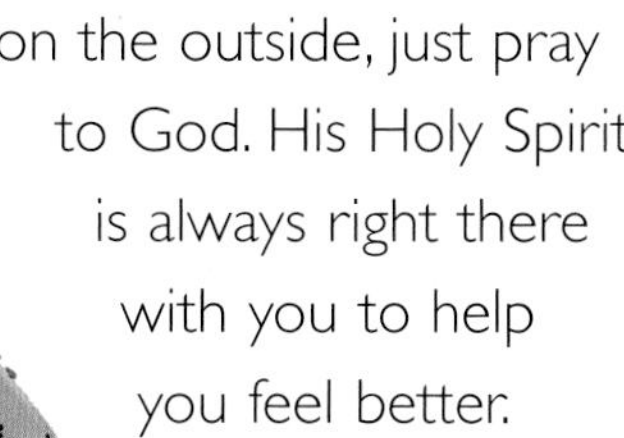

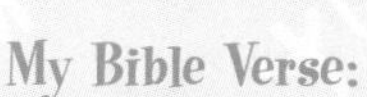

My Bible Verse:
The Holy Spirit helps us with our daily problems.
Romans 8:26, TLB

My Prayer:
When I am hurt and need someone
to care,
I'm glad, dear God, that your Spirit
is there.

18
JUNE

Share with Others

Who is Kaitlyn sharing with? God is happy when we share what we have with our friends. But many other people need food and clothes and toys. You won't be able to help them all, but you can share your things with some of the people in your neighborhood. Or you can share your money with some people who live far away. When you share with others, God will bless you and give you what you need.

My Bible Verse:
A generous person will be blessed because he shares his food with the poor. Proverbs 22:9, ICB

My Prayer:
Help me, Lord, to share with those
Who might need extra food or
clothes.

Everything Belongs to God

19
JUNE

When you go outdoors you can see birds and bushes and beautiful flowers. You might even see a bee or a butterfly. What other things do you see outdoors? Every plant, every animal, every bug, and every bird on the ground or in the sky belongs to God because he made it. Do you see any people? They belong to God too. God owns everything in the whole world.

My Bible Verse:

The earth is the Lord's, and everything in it. The world and all its people belong to him.
Psalm 24:1, NLT

My Prayer:

You own the world from the sky to
the ground—
All that I see when I look around.

20
JUNE

Peaceful Places

Shh! Jack is sleeping. He found a quiet, peaceful place to take a nap. He knows it can be hard to take a nap where it's loud or noisy. Where do you like to take naps? Jack took his teddy bear with him. What do you take with you when it's time to sleep? Did you know that Jesus is always with you too? Jesus helps you feel calm and peaceful anytime—even when it's loud or noisy!

My Bible Verse:
My people will live in peaceful places. They will have safe homes. They will live in calm places of rest. Isaiah 32:18, ICB

My Prayer:
Jesus, your love is always the best. You give me peaceful places to rest.

Lots to Learn

21 JUNE

Parker always has lots of questions. He wonders about the clouds in the sky. He wants to know how the ocean waves go up and down. Do you ever wonder about things? We can learn many things from reading books. We can learn many things from our parents and teachers. But God can help us learn and understand more than anyone else. God can help you learn about his love and the special plans he has for you. When you pray, ask God to help you learn and understand.

My Bible Verse:

Wisdom begins with respect for the Lord. And understanding begins with knowing God, the Holy One.
Proverbs 9:10, ICB

My Prayer:

Dear God, please help me to
understand
All about you and your special
plans.

22 JUNE

We Are Different

Did you know that fish come in all different colors, shapes, and sizes? Boys and girls come in all different colors, shapes, and sizes too. That's the way God wants it to be. He created us so we would all be different from one another. Some people try to change themselves to be more like someone else. God doesn't want us to try to be like other people. God wants us to be more like him.

My Bible Verse:

Do not change yourselves to be like the people of this world.
Romans 12:2, ICB

My Prayer:

Thank you, God, for making us all—
All colors and shapes, both short and tall.

Walk in the Light

23
JUNE

These kids are going for a walk. Have you ever tried walking in the dark? You can't see where you are going. You bump into things and trip or fall. People who don't believe in God are like people who walk in the dark. They don't know where they are going. But when you believe in God, he shows you where he wants you to go. When you do what God wants, it's like walking in the light.

My Bible Verse:
Let us walk in the light of the Lord! Isaiah 2:5, NLT

My Prayer:
Lord, I want to walk in your light. Show me how to do what is right.

24 JUNE

Look for Jesus

"Come on, Jack!" says Zoë. "Let's go find our friends!" Have you ever looked for someone? Were you happy when you found that person? The Bible tells us that when we look for Jesus, he will be good to us. Jesus wants us to look for him every day. You can find Jesus when you listen to Bible stories. You can find Jesus when you pray. Jesus is easy to find when you know where to look!

My Bible Verse:

The Lord is good to those whose hope is in him, to the one who seeks him. Lamentations 3:25, NIV

My Prayer:

I never need to look very far. Jesus, I know right where you are.

Squeaky Clean

25
JUNE

Kaitlyn is taking a bath. She wants her body to be squeaky clean. Do you like your body to be squeaky clean? Did you know that you can clean your body on the inside, too? When we disobey God, the wrong things we do are called sins. When we sin, we feel dirty on the inside. But if we tell God we are sorry, he takes away our sin. It's like taking a bath on the inside.

My Bible Verse:
Take away my sin, and I will be clean. Wash me, and I will be whiter than snow. Psalm 51:7, ICB

My Prayer:
Lord, please take away my sin,
So I'll be clean both outside and in.

26 JUNE

Good Friends

Jack has lots of good friends. His friends are Zoë, Kaitlyn, and Parker. He even has his dog for a friend! Do you have a good friend? A good friend will love you no matter what happens. Even on a bad day, a good friend will care about you and try to help you. Everybody wants to have a good friend. But it is also important to be a good friend. Can you be a good friend to someone today?

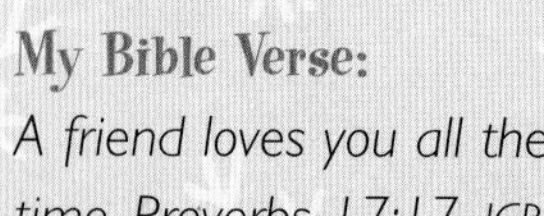

My Bible Verse:
A friend loves you all the time. Proverbs 17:17, ICB

My Prayer:
Help me, Lord, to be a good friend
All day long, from beginning to end.

Rainbows and Promises

27
JUNE

When Noah came out of the ark, God put a rainbow in the sky. It was a sign of God's promise to never cover the whole world with water again. When God makes a promise, he always keeps it. God gives us many promises in the Bible. He promises to love us and take care of us. He promises to hear us when we pray. Are you glad God keeps his promises? The next time you see a rainbow in the sky, what will you think about? Will you remember that God keeps his promises?

My Bible Verse:

The Lord will keep his promises. With love he takes care of all he has made. Psalm 145:13, ICB

My Prayer:

Thanks for each promise from long ago
And for the love that you always show.

28 JUNE

Without Being Told

Zoë and Kaitlyn are picking up their toys even though no one told them to. They have learned that they are supposed to pick up their toys when they are done playing. Have you learned to pick up your toys? Have you learned to say please and thank you? Have you learned to be a helper? What can you do today without being told to do it?

My Bible Verse:

We must be sure to obey the truth we have learned already.
Philippians 3:16, NLT

My Prayer:

Help me to do the things I should do
Even if no one tells me to.

Set It Free

29

JUNE

Jack caught a butterfly in his jar. But that is not where a butterfly belongs. Jack set it free so it could fly away and be happy. When we do things that are wrong, we're like a butterfly in a jar. We need to be set free from the wrong things. Those sins keep us from being happy. When we're sorry, Jesus takes away our sins and makes us free. Then we can live the way God wants us to live and be happy!

My Bible Verse:

You have been set free from sin. Romans 6:18, NIrV

My Prayer:

Thank you, Jesus, for setting me free
And taking my sin away from me.

30 JUNE

God's Comfort

Zoë loves her big, fluffy pillows. And she loves her big, fluffy dog. She likes to cuddle and snuggle and be comfortable. Do you have something that is big and fluffy? Does it give you comfort? When we pray to God, he can comfort us too. He can help us with our problems. He can make us feel safe. God's love comforts us. It's the most comforting thing there is!

My Bible Verse:

What a wonderful God we have . . . the one who so wonderfully comforts and strengthens us.
2 Corinthians 1:3, TLB

My Prayer:

When I need your comfort and love,
You send it down from heaven above.

July

1 JULY

A House on the Rocks

Did you ever build a house in the sand? Rain washes the sand away, and down goes the house! Jesus told about a man who built a real house on sand. Rain came down and the house fell flat. Another man built his house on rocks. It rained, but the rocks stayed in place and the house stood tall. Jesus said that if we obey him, we're like the man who built his house on the rocks. When troubles come, we'll be strong.

My Bible Verse:

Anyone who listens to my teaching and obeys me is wise, like a person who builds a house on solid rock.
Matthew 7:24, NLT

My Prayer:

I'll obey you, dear God, and then I'll
be strong.
You'll help me when troubles start
coming along.

Don't Brag

2 JULY

How tall is Kaitlyn? She is much taller than Zoë. But just because Kaitlyn is taller than Zoë, that doesn't mean she is better. Are you bigger than one of your friends? Being bigger or smarter or stronger is not something to brag or boast about. God made us in all different sizes. And we can all do different things. God doesn't want us to brag about ourselves. If you want to be proud, be proud about all the good things that God does for you every day.

My Bible Verse:
The person who wishes to boast should boast only of what the Lord has done.
I Corinthians 1:31, NLT

My Prayer:
Oh, Lord, please help me not to boast,
But do the things that please you most.

3

JULY

Say Good Things

Jack is telling Parker a secret. Do you ever tell secrets? Good secrets are okay. Maybe Jack is going to do something nice, like surprise his sister and give her a gift. Do you think Jack is talking about Zoë? It's okay to talk about others if you say good things. But it's wrong to tell a lie about someone else. And it's wrong to say something unkind about another person. If you say good things about others, they will say good things about you.

My Bible Verse:

He doesn't tell lies about others. He doesn't do wrong to his neighbors. He doesn't say anything bad about them.
Psalm 15:3, NIrV

My Prayer:

Help me, Lord Jesus, in all that I say,
To talk about others in the right way.

Tell Your Children

4
JULY

Jack and Zoë like to listen to the stories Kaitlyn reads. They also like to listen to stories their grandma tells. Does your grandma ever tell you stories about when she was a little girl? Does she tell about prayers God has answered? It's fun to listen to those stories, isn't it? God wants parents and grandparents to tell their children about the things God has done for them. Then the children will learn how great God is. When you grow up, you can tell your children about God too.

My Bible Verse:

We will tell [our children] about what the Lord has done. . . . We will talk about his power and the wonderful things he has done.
Psalm 78:4, NIrV

My Prayer:

Thank you for stories from long ago
That tell of your love so children will know.

5

JULY

Pleasing God

Kaitlyn is happy to be outside on a warm, sunny day. She wants to do what is right and please God today. Do you know how to please God? If you do what God says in the Bible, you will please God. He wants you to be kind to your friends and to do what your parents ask. He wants you to pray and sing happy songs for him. When you obey God, it's like following in his steps. Following God is the best way to be happy!

My Bible Verse:

When a man's steps follow the Lord, God is pleased with his ways. Psalm 37:23, ICB

My Prayer:

Help me, Lord, to please you today,
To walk in your steps and try to obey.

Give Cheerfully

6
JULY

It looks like Zoë is giving her fish away. Do you ever give things away? Maybe you give away your shoes or clothes when you outgrow them. Even though you can't wear them anymore, they may still be special to you. Do you ever give your toys to children who don't have any? Sometimes it's hard to give our things to someone else. But God wants us to be happy about giving to others. When we give cheerfully, it makes God happy too!

My Bible Verse:

God loves the person
who gives cheerfully.
2 Corinthians 9:7, NLT

My Prayer:

Jesus, please help me to truly care
And cheerfully give when it's time
to share.

7

JULY

Be Gentle

Kaitlyn is caring for her animal friends. She is being gentle with them. Being gentle means being careful not to hurt others. Have you ever held a baby? Did you ever pet a kitten or a puppy? You were probably told to be gentle. When we are gentle with others, it shows that we love them. And do you know what? God is gentle with you because he loves you so much!

My Bible Verse:

Be completely gentle. Be patient. Put up with one another in love.
Ephesians 4:2, NIrV

My Prayer:

Help me, Lord, to be gentle like you
And treat others kindly the way that you do.

Open My Eyes

8 JULY

Parker is trying to read the Bible. He can understand some of the words, but not all of them. It's hard to understand everything that the Bible says. But there are many wonderful stories in the Bible. Every time we read the Bible or listen to a story from it, we will understand a little more. Understanding what God says in the Bible is like being able to see well. Ask God to open your eyes to help you see and understand his words.

My Bible Verse:

Open my eyes so that I can see the wonderful truths in your law. Psalm 119:18, NIrV

My Prayer:

Lord, help me to understand and see
The stories and lessons you have for me.

9

JULY

More than the Birds

Zoë is looking at a pretty little hummingbird. Have you ever seen how fast a hummingbird's wings go back and forth? That keeps it in one place in the air. Then it uses its long beak to suck a sweet drink from flowers. God takes care of the birds and helps them find food because he loves them. But God loves you even more than the birds. So of course God will take care of you, too!

My Bible Verse:

Your heavenly Father feeds the birds. And you know that you are worth much more than the birds.
Matthew 6:26, ICB

My Prayer:

Jesus, you love the birds in the air,
So I know you'll keep me in your care.

How High?

10
JULY

Parker is flying a kite. It's going higher and higher into the sky. How high can you reach? Can you measure how high? A kite can go higher than that, but the clouds are even higher. And after the clouds, there is more sky. The sky goes so high that no one can measure it. The Bible says that God's love is higher than the skies above. That means that God loves you more than anyone can measure.

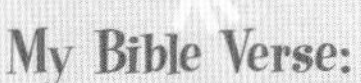

My Bible Verse:
Great is your love. It is higher than the heavens. Psalm 108:4, NIrV

My Prayer:
Oh, God, your love is very high. It reaches higher than the sky.

11 JULY

Be Holy

Did you know that God can't do anything that's wrong? He can't sin. So God is holy. He is perfect. The angels in Zoë's picture are not as holy as God. And people do wrong things, so we're not as holy as God. But because God loves us, he will forgive us for our sins. When we tell God we are sorry, he will take our sin away and make us holy like him.

My Bible Verse:

God called us to be holy and does not want us to live in sin.
1 Thessalonians 4:7, ICB

My Prayer:

Lord, please take my sin away.
Make me holy like you, I pray.

Act like Jesus

JULY

Jack and Kaitlyn are making pictures. They are talking and sharing and being kind to each other. They are acting the way Jesus acted. Jesus loved and cared about others. Jesus helped people who needed help. Jesus obeyed God, his Father in heaven. Every time you obey and do what is right, you are acting like Jesus. What are some ways you can obey and act like Jesus?

My Bible Verse:
In your lives you must think and act like Christ Jesus.
Philippians 2:5, ICB

My Prayer:
Jesus, I want to act like you
In all I say and all I do.

13 JULY

Push Ahead

Jack is taking his friends for a ride. They are looking forward to a fun day. Are you going to have a fun day today? Everyone has bad days. Sometimes they are bad because we do bad things. But you can forget about all the bad things that are behind you. And you can ask God to help you push ahead to a happy day.

My Bible Verse:

Here is the one thing I do. I forget what is behind me. I push hard toward what is ahead of me. Philippians 3:13, NIrV

My Prayer:

Help me forget all the bad days
I've had,
'Cause I want to be happy today,
not sad.

Close By

14
JULY

Zoë loves being close to her big sheepdog. He will keep her safe from the little mouse and help her not to feel afraid. Do you like to be close to someone? You can't always be close to a big dog. You can't always be close to your mom or dad. But the Bible says that God is always close by your side. He'll help you to not feel afraid. He'll keep you safe from anything that's bad.

My Bible Verse:
I know the Lord is always with me. I will not be shaken, for he is right beside me. Psalm 16:8, NLT

My Prayer:
Dear God, I never have to fear.
You keep me safe—you're always near.

15 JULY

Help with Problems

Oh, no! Parker and Jack have a big problem! They are trying to help move the dog, but he's too heavy. Even when we try to help others, we can still have problems. Even when we obey God and do what is right, we can have problems. Even if we learn a lot about Jesus, we can still have problems. God never said that we won't have problems. But he does promise to help us when we do.

My Bible Verse:

People who do what is right may have many problems. But the Lord will solve them all.
Psalm 34:19, ICB

My Prayer:

Lord, thank you that you will help
me today
If problems or troubles come my way.

The Whole World

16
JULY

Kaitlyn and Zoë are looking at a big map. Have you ever seen a map? A map shows that there are many faraway places in the world. The Bible tells us that God loves everyone in the whole world. He loves everyone so much that he sent his Son, Jesus, to die on the cross. Jesus died for everyone in the whole world. But then he came back to life! Everyone who believes in Jesus will go to heaven someday to be with him.

My Bible Verse:

For God so loved the world that he gave his only Son, so that everyone who believes in him will not perish but have eternal life. John 3:16, NLT

My Prayer:

Thank you, God, for your wonderful love,
And for your Son, Jesus, sent from above.

17

JULY

Need Directions?

Oops! Jack made a wrong turn, and now he isn't quite sure where to go. Should he go left or right? Have you ever needed someone to tell you which way to go? Have you ever needed someone to tell you what to do? Sometimes it's hard to make the right choices. But God will help us when we're not sure what to do or where to go. And God's directions are always just right!

My Bible Verse:

I am the Lord your God. . . . I direct you in the way you should go. Isaiah 48:17, NIrV

My Prayer:

Help me, Lord, to always know
Exactly where I need to go.

God Forgives

18
JULY

The children are sending notes up to God with their balloons. What do you think the notes say? You don't have to send notes. You can just talk to God. You can tell him you are sorry when you do something wrong. When you tell him you are sorry, God will forgive you. That's because he loves you very much.

My Bible Verse:

Lord, you are good. You are forgiving. You are full of love for all who call out to you.
Psalm 86:5, NIrV

My Prayer:

Forgive me, Lord, when I do
something wrong.
Your love makes me feel like
singing a song!

19 JULY

God's Words

Jack is looking at a big book. It's the Bible. Jack wants to read the Bible because it is from God. Maybe if Jack doesn't know all the words, someone will read it to him. Do you ever look at the Bible? The Bible is full of God's words. In the Bible God tells us how we can obey him. In the Bible God tells us how we can be happy. In the Bible God tells us how much he loves us. It's the best book in the whole world! Ask God to help you understand his words so you can obey him and be happy.

My Bible Verse:

Help me understand, so
I can obey your teachings.
Psalm 119:34, ICB

My Prayer:

Thank you for words that come
from you.
Lord, I know your words are true.

God's Riches

20
JULY

Kaitlyn is enjoying a warm summer day. She found a soft, shady spot and she's eating some tasty berries. All these wonderful things are rich gifts from God. God has many gifts that he wants to share with you. Good food and warm sunshine and gentle breezes all come from God. Can you think of some more riches that he shares with us? Remember to say thank you to God for all his great riches.

My Bible Verse:
Yes, God's riches are very great! God's wisdom and knowledge have no end! Romans 11:33, ICB

My Prayer:
Lord, thank you for gifts I see everywhere.
Thank you for all of the riches you share.

21

JULY

Look to the Hills

What do you think Kaitlyn is looking for? Maybe she is looking for some help. Where do you look when you need help? Do you look in a book? Do you look for your mom or dad? The Bible tells us to look at the hills. They can't help us. But God can. He made the hills! If God is great enough to create the hills and everything else on the earth, he is great enough to help you with whatever you need.

My Bible Verse:

I lift up my eyes to the hills—
where does my help come from?
My help comes from the Lord,
the Maker of heaven and earth.
Psalm 121:1-2, NIV

My Prayer:

Lord, you created the hills that I see,
So I know that you can always help me.

Don't Stumble

22
JULY

Zoë is running up the hill. She is being careful so she won't trip and fall. Did you ever tumble down when you were running fast? It's important to watch where you are going. It's important to be careful how we act, too. God's words in the Bible teach us to be careful. God helps us to be wise and do what's right. He helps us keep on doing good, kind things.

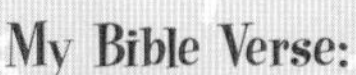

My Bible Verse:
When you walk, nothing will slow you down. When you run, you won't trip and fall.
Proverbs 4:12, NIrV

My Prayer:
Lord, please help me not to fall,
For you can help me most of all.

23 JULY

Day and Night

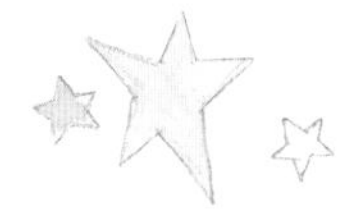

Look at that Parker! He should be going to bed, but he loves to count. Now he is counting the little lambs tucked under the blanket. Parker likes to think about things during the day and the night. It seems like he never stops! What do you like to think about? It's good to think about things. And it's especially good to think about God all day and all night. We should never stop thinking about God and his love for us.

My Bible Verse:
Lord, during the night I remember who you are.
Psalm 119:55, NIrV

My Prayer:
Dear God, I think of you day and night. You love me and help me to do what is right.

No More Worries

24 JULY

Poor Zoë! She is so worried. Her bear has an owie. But Kaitlyn will help her fix it. Do you ever worry about things? Do you worry about being left with a babysitter? Do you worry about being alone in the dark? Do you worry about noises you hear? Whenever you are worried, God wants you to pray to him. He wants you to tell him about your worries. Then God will take care of everything.

My Bible Verse:

Turn all your worries over to him. He cares about you.
1 Peter 5:7, NIrV

My Prayer:

Jesus, if I start to worry,
I promise to pray to you in a hurry.

25 JULY

It Shows

Jack and Kaitlyn are watching a beautiful sunset by the sea. Have you ever seen the sun go down behind a lake or ocean? Everything that God made is so beautiful. The sun and the sea and the mountains and the sky show how great God is. Everyone in the whole world can know about the greatness of God by looking at everything he made. Wherever you look, God's greatness shows.

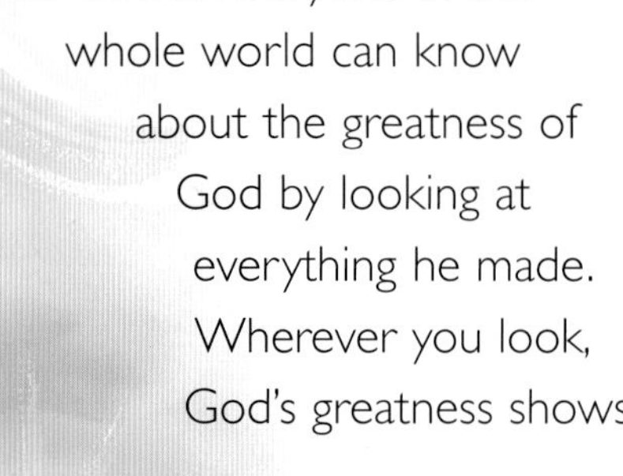

My Bible Verse:

People everywhere will know the Lord's greatness. This news will spread like water covering the sea. Habakkuk 2:14, ICB

My Prayer:

Oh, God, I see how great you are
Wherever I look, near or far.

Noah Obeyed

26
JULY

Look at Kaitlyn and Jack in the little boat. Do you know the story about Noah and his BIG boat? A long time ago, people became very bad. God decided to wash everything away with a flood and start over again. But Noah loved God. So God told him to build a big boat and take the animals inside. Noah did exactly what God told him to do. So Noah and his family and the animals were safe during the Flood because Noah obeyed God.

My Bible Verse:
Noah did everything exactly as God had commanded him.
Genesis 6:22, NLT

My Prayer:
Lord, just like Noah, I want to obey
And listen to all the words you say.

27 JULY

A Noisy Night

Jack was sleeping, but he woke up. He heard the wind blowing and the thunder rumbling. Jack was afraid. But then he prayed. And he remembered that God was watching over him. So Jack went back to sleep. Can you think of times when you might be afraid? When you feel afraid, you can ask God to take care of you. He'll help you remember that he watches over you all the time, even during a thunderstorm.

My Bible Verse:

When I am afraid, I put my trust in you. Psalm 56:3, NLT

My Prayer:

Lord, please keep me safe and warm,
Even through a thunderstorm.

Depend on God

28
JULY

Kaitlyn's cat is afraid. But Kaitlyn isn't. She's depending on the hammock her daddy made. She knows it won't fall. Do you depend on your parents to do everything they can to keep you safe? When you depend on someone, you don't need to worry about things. The Bible tells us to depend on God. He promises to take care of everything for us. And God always keeps his promises.

My Bible Verse:
You will find peace and rest when you turn away from your sins and depend on me.
Isaiah 30:15, NIrV

My Prayer:
Teach me, Lord, to depend on you
To keep me safe and happy, too.

29
JULY

God Decides

Kaitlyn was using her umbrella because it was raining. But now the sun is shining! Have you ever seen the weather change suddenly? Sometimes it can be cold in the morning and warm in the afternoon. Sometimes it can be sunny in the morning and cloudy in the afternoon. God decides what the weather is going to be each day. God decides many other things too. That's because God always knows what is best.

My Bible Verse:
The Lord does whatever pleases him, in the heavens and on the earth. Psalm 135:6, NIV

My Prayer:
Lord, you can make it rain or shine. What you decide will be just fine!

Saying Thank You

30
JULY

Jack gave Parker a gift for his birthday. "Thank you, Jack!" said Parker. Do you ever get presents? Do you remember to say thank you? It's important to say thank you when someone gives you a gift. Did you know that God gives us presents every day? He gives us our home and food. He gives us sunshine and rain. Those are all gifts! Remember to say thank you to God for everything he gives you every day.

My Bible Verse:

Always give thanks to God the Father for everything, in the name of our Lord Jesus Christ.
Ephesians 5:20, ICB

My Prayer:

Thank you, God, for gifts you send.
In Jesus' name I pray. Amen.

31 JULY

Filled with Joy

Kaitlyn is so happy! Do you know why? She knows that Jesus loves her! She's filled with joy. That means she's happy on the inside. Jesus is the only one who can fill us with joy. He can give us joy even when we have problems. Jesus cares for us and shows us how he wants us to live. If you want to be filled with joy, ask Jesus to come into your heart. The joy that Jesus gives on the inside will show on the outside!

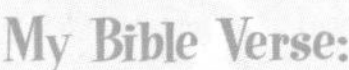

My Bible Verse:

Even though you have not seen [Jesus], you love him. . . . You are filled with a glorious joy that can't be put into words.

1 Peter 1:8, NIrV

My Prayer:

Jesus, you give lots of joy
To every girl and every boy.

August

1

AUGUST

Be Happy with What You Have

Some of the kids in this picture may have many things. And some of them may not have as much. But God wants us to be happy with what we have. If we always want more and more, we will never be happy. God will give you the food and clothes and toys you need. So be happy with what you have. And don't worry about what you don't have.

My Bible Verse:

It is better to be happy with what you have than always to be wanting more.
Ecclesiastes 6:9, ICB

My Prayer:

Lord, you give me all that I need.
Help me to be happy indeed!

God Is Near

Parker looks up and sees ladybugs and bluebirds in the sky. He wonders where God is. Sometimes God seems far away. Does it seem to you like God is far away?

The Bible tells us that God is NOT far away! God is near you when you listen to his words in the Bible. God is near you when you talk to him in prayer. Whenever you want to feel close to God, just call out to him. Then you will know that he is right there.

My Bible Verse:
The Lord is near to all who call on him. Psalm 145:18, NIV

My Prayer:
Dear God, I know that you are near me. I know that you will always hear me.

3 AUGUST

A Bug Is a Bug

Parker wonders why he is Parker. He wonders why bugs are bugs and turtles are turtles. If you could be anything you wanted to be, what might that be? A butterfly that flies in the sky? A tiny bug that can crawl anywhere? Or a huge animal like an elephant? Guess what? God created you to be exactly what he wanted you to be. He created bugs to be bugs, boys to be boys, and girls to be girls.

My Bible Verse:

Everything that happens was planned long ago. A man is only what he was created to be.
Ecclesiastes 6:10, ICB

My Prayer:

Thank you, God, for creating me
Exactly how I'm supposed to be.

By His Power

4
AUGUST

Jack is flying his kite on a sunny afternoon. He is enjoying the fresh air and the warm sunshine. He likes looking up into God's big blue sky. God made everything from the sky to the ground. He made it all because he is so powerful. Only God is great enough to create the world and everything in it. And because God loves you, he made it all for you to enjoy.

Oh, Lord God, you made the skies and the earth. You made them with your very great power.
Jeremiah 32:17, ICB

My Prayer:

Thank you for making the earth and
the skies
And all that I see in front of my eyes.

5 AUGUST

Love One Another

Kaitlyn is giving Jack and Zoë a big hug. She loves them very much. Love is a special gift from God. Do you love your parents? Do you have a brother or sister you love? You can show your love for others by being kind and helpful—and by giving them hugs! Remember to TELL your family and friends that you love them too. And when you pray, don't forget to tell God that you love him.

My Bible Verse:
Dear friends, let us love one another, because love comes from God. 1 John 4:7, NIrV

My Prayer:
Thank you, God, for the love you send
So I can love you, my family, my friends.

Don't Be Proud

6
AUGUST

Do you see the big cat in the picture? He could think that he's better than the other animals because he's bigger. He could act proud. But he knows that's not a good idea. So he's helping to clean the bird's face by licking it. He's being a kind and helpful friend. God made everyone special. He doesn't want any of us to think we're better than someone else. No matter how big we are or what we can do, God loves us all the same.

My Bible Verse:
Don't be proud. Be gentle and patient. Colossians 3:12, NIrV

My Prayer:
All people, Lord, are special to you. Help me to see them as special too!

7
AUGUST

Be Kind

Parker and Zoë have a little caterpillar friend that needs a home. They want to be kind to the little guy so he doesn't get hurt. There are many ways that you can be kind to people who need something. You can hold the door open for your mom. You can let your sister have the last piece of candy. You can make a picture for your grandma. Can you think of other kind things you can do? When we are kind to those who need our help, it makes us feel happy inside.

My Bible Verse:
Being kind to the needy brings happiness. Proverbs 14:21, ICB

My Prayer:
Jesus, I know you'll help me to find
Things I can do that are helpful
and kind.

Wise Words

8
AUGUST

Zoë is whispering something to Jack. What do you think she is saying? Do you ever whisper to your friends? The Bible tells us to say things that are wise. Wise words are helpful. Wise words are kind. Wise words are truthful. Wise words make others happy. What wise words can you say today?

My Bible Verse:
A good person says wise things.
Proverbs 10:31, ICB

My Prayer:
Lord, I want to say words that are wise,
To say what's kind and never tell lies.

9 AUGUST

A Happy Morning

Parker is happy for a brand-new day. He can hardly wait to get out of bed and go exploring. Maybe he will find some special leaves. Maybe he will catch a grasshopper. But first he will thank God for the new day. Do you wake up happy in the morning? Every new day is a gift from God. When you wake up in the morning, smile and say thank you to God.

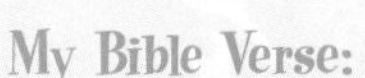

My Bible Verse:

This is the day the Lord has made. We will rejoice and be glad in it. Psalm 118:24, NLT

My Prayer:

Thank you, Lord, for a brand-new day.
I'm happy that I can work and play.

Just like the Sun

10
AUGUST

Kaitlyn is looking out of her window. She is glad to see that the sun is shining. We need the sun. The sun gives us light. The sun keeps us warm. The sun helps everything to grow. The Bible says that God is like the sun. We need God, too. He gives us everything we need—even his love—and he keeps us safe.

My Bible Verse:
The Lord God is like the sun that gives us light. He is like a shield that keeps us safe.
Psalm 84:11, NIrV

My Prayer:
Lord, I need sunshine, and I need you. Thanks for the sun and your love for me too.

11 AUGUST

Another Home

Jack just learned that he has more than one home. He has the home he is living in now. And he has another home in heaven that Jesus is getting ready for him. Someday Jesus will come back from heaven. Then he will take us to live with him forever. That will be a very happy day for everyone who believes in Jesus. You will have many happy days in your home on earth. But you will have many more happy days in your home in heaven.

My Bible Verse:

Our homeland is in heaven, and we are waiting for our Savior, the Lord Jesus Christ, to come from heaven. Philippians 3:20, ICB

My Prayer:

Someday, Jesus, you'll come from the sky
To take us to your home on high.

I Feel like Singing

12 AUGUST

Kaitlyn is going for a walk. She's whistling because she's happy. She knows she isn't alone. God is with her! Did you know that wherever you go, God goes with you? You can't see him, but he's always there. He watches over you and protects you. God will help you and keep you safe. You don't have to be afraid. Doesn't that make you feel like singing?

My Bible Verse:
You are my help. Because of your protection, I sing.
Psalm 63:7, ICB

My Prayer:
Lord, you protect me from everything bad.
I want to sing, 'cause your help makes me glad.

13 AUGUST

Choose Good Friends

Parker is picking only good apples from the tree. If he picked a rotten apple, it could ruin the apple pie his mom wants to make. Did you know that friends are like apples? All it takes is one bad friend to ruin your day. A bad friend can talk you into doing things you know you shouldn't do. A bad friend can get you into trouble. Ask God to help you choose friends that will be good for you.

My Bible Verse:

Some friends may ruin you. But a real friend will be more loyal than a brother.
Proverbs 18:24, ICB

My Prayer:

I want to play with friends
who are good,
Who help me to live the way
that I should.

Be Blessed

14 AUGUST

Parker and Jack are blessed. Do you know what that means? It means they are happy. It means that they have everything they need. When we love Jesus and obey him, he blesses us. We are blessed with family and friends. We are blessed with food and clothes. We are blessed because we know that God loves us and will take care of us. Do you want to be blessed? Believe in Jesus, and he will bless you, too!

My Bible Verse:

The person who trusts in the Lord will be blessed. The Lord will show him that he can be trusted.
Jeremiah 17:7, ICB

My Prayer:

Jesus, you give the very best. Because of you, I'm happy and blessed.

15

AUGUST

Remember Special Times

Do you know what kind of book this is? It's a book where you keep pictures. Do you have one like it? Pictures help us remember special times like birthday parties or trips to the zoo. Stories help us remember special times too. Bible stories tell how God made the world. Bible stories tell about when Jesus was born. Bible stories tell how we can believe in Jesus. The Bible is a very special book!

My Bible Verse:

These are written so that you may believe that Jesus is the Messiah, the Son of God, and that by believing in him you will have life. John 20:31, NLT

My Prayer:

Thanks for the Bible, which helps me know
About special times from long ago.

Think about God

16
AUGUST

Look at the animals sleeping. What do you suppose they are thinking about? What do you think about at night when it's dark? Do you try to remember that God is right there with you? At night, when the lights go out, you can think about God. You can imagine him in heaven looking down at you while you are sleeping in your bed. Thinking about God will help you feel peaceful and safe. Then you can have happy dreams!

My Bible Verse:
I remember you while I'm lying in bed. I think about you through the night. Psalm 63:6, ICB

My Prayer:
Lord, when I think about you at night, I know that I'm going to be all right.

17
AUGUST

Fill It Up!

Jack and Kaitlyn are filling up the wagon with apples. Do you think they can fill it to the top? What do you like to put in your wagon? God gives us so many good things, it's easy to fill up a wagon! He gives us lots of good food and clothes. He also gives us books and toys. He even gives us family and friends. God fills our lives with his love, all the way up to the top!

My Bible Verse:
The earth is filled with your love, O Lord. Psalm 119:64, NIV

My Prayer:
Lord, you fill my life to the top.
Your love and goodness never stop.

Which Way?

Jack is confused. There are too many signs. He doesn't know which way to go. Life can be confusing too. Sometimes it's hard to know the right things to do and the right places to go. But if you love God and learn what he says in the Bible, he will help you. And God will always answer you when you pray. If you love God, he'll help you obey him. And you won't be confused.

My Bible Verse:
Love the Lord your God, walk in all his ways, obey his commands.
Joshua 22:5, NLT

My Prayer:
If I learn your words and pray
every day,
I know you will guide me and
show me the way.

19 AUGUST

Listen Up!

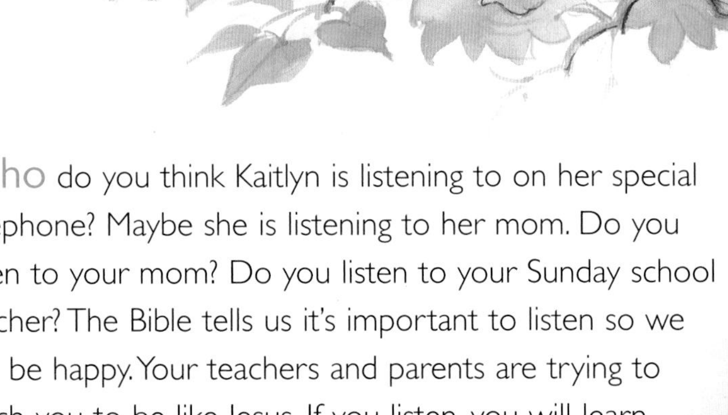

Who do you think Kaitlyn is listening to on her special telephone? Maybe she is listening to her mom. Do you listen to your mom? Do you listen to your Sunday school teacher? The Bible tells us it's important to listen so we can be happy. Your teachers and parents are trying to teach you to be like Jesus. If you listen, you will learn to do the right things. And that will make you happy.

My Bible Verse:

Now, my children, listen to me. Those who follow my ways are happy. Proverbs 8:32, ICB

My Prayer:

Help me, Lord, to listen to you
And to my parents and teachers, too.

Look in the Sky

20
AUGUST

Parker is looking up into the sky. He can see for miles and miles with his binoculars. Have you ever looked into the sky? Did you see the sun and the clouds? Did you see birds or a rainbow? God created everything you saw. A person could never make any of those things. Only God could. Isn't he wonderful?

My Bible Verse:
Look up toward the sky. Who created everything you see?
Isaiah 40:26, NIrV

My Prayer:
Oh, God, you created the sun way up high,
And all that I see when I look in the sky.

21 AUGUST

A Message

Kaitlyn is reading a message. Did you ever get a message? Maybe your grandma sent you a card or someone mailed you a picture. But did you know that the Bible is full of the most important messages of all? They're from God! One of the messages says that God is light. That means that he is good, and he can light up the way for us. We can trust everything that God says. God's light helps us see how we should act. Maybe you can share this message with a friend.

My Bible Verse:

Here is the message we have heard from him and announce to you. God is light. There is no darkness in him at all.

1 John 1:5, NIrV

My Prayer:

Lord, you are good and full of light. You help me do the things that are right.

Lift up Your Hands

22
AUGUST

When we pray, we often fold our hands, close our eyes, and bow our heads. This shows that we honor God for being so special. But it's okay to be excited about God too. Kaitlyn, Jack, and Parker are excited about the tomatoes and flowers God helped them grow. They are lifting up their hands and shouting, "Thank you!" and "I love you, God!" Would you like to lift up your hands? God always enjoys hearing from you no matter how you pray!

My Bible Verse:

Let's lift up our hands to God in heaven. Let's pray to him with all our hearts.
Lamentations 3:41, NIrV

My Prayer:

Dear Lord, I know you're always there,
No matter how I say my prayer.

23 AUGUST

Work Hard

Zoë has been working hard all afternoon. She picked some corn to take home for dinner. You can work hard too. Working hard can be fun. You can pick up your toys. You can put your dirty clothes in the laundry basket. What other things can you do? The Bible says that people who work hard are happy. When people work hard, God blesses them with good things.

My Bible Verse:

Lazy people want much but get little, but those who work hard will prosper and be satisfied.
Proverbs 13:4, NLT

My Prayer:

I may be young, but I can work hard,
Inside my house or out in my yard.

Honor Each Other

24 AUGUST

It's time to take turns playing with the toys! Have you ever had to take turns? Have you ever let someone else be first? The Bible says to honor others. So we should be happy to share and take turns. If you always try to be first, others won't want to play with you. But if you treat your friends like they're special, they'll know that you love them.

My Bible Verse:

Love each other deeply. Honor others more than yourselves.
Romans 12:10, NIrV

My Prayer:

Help me to treat all my friends with love,
The same way you share your love from above.

25 AUGUST

Fruit Trees

Do you think Zoë will find some apples on the peach tree? Of course not! Only peaches grow on peach trees. The Bible says that we're like fruit trees. If we do good things, others will know we love Jesus. But if we do bad things, others will think we don't love Jesus. So be sure to do good things. These good things are like fruit. They will show what kind of person you are.

My Bible Verse:

Each tree is known by its fruit.
Luke 6:44, ICB

My Prayer:

I'll try to be good so others can see
I love you, Jesus, and you love me!

Keep Growing

Zoë is trying to find out if she's grown an inch or two. Do you ever measure yourself to see if you've grown? Your body isn't the only thing that grows. Your mind can grow too. It doesn't get bigger. It just gets filled with more stuff. Eating good food makes your body get bigger. But listening to Bible stories and learning Bible verses fills your mind with good things about Jesus. Your love for him will grow as you grow to know him more!

My Bible Verse:

Grow in the grace of our Lord and Savior Jesus Christ. Get to know him better.

2 Peter 3:18, NIrV

My Prayer:

Dear God, please help my mind to grow.
There's so much more I want to know.

27 AUGUST

Like Raindrops

Kaitlyn and Zoë are enjoying big, wet raindrops. Do you like to watch the rain come down? God sends rain to water the earth. Rain helps the grass and flowers to grow. Rain makes everything fresh and clean. God's words in the Bible are like that too. They help us grow to be like Jesus. They tell us how we can be clean from sin. You can enjoy God's words, just like you enjoy big, wet raindrops.

My Bible Verse:

Let my teaching fall like rain. Let my words come down like dew. Let them be like raindrops on new grass.
Deuteronomy 32:2, NIrV

My Prayer:

Oh, Lord, your words are fresh
and clean
Like rain that makes the grass
so green.

Only One God

28 AUGUST

There are many things for Jack to learn. Sometimes he has to say, "I don't know!" Do you like to learn new things? There is something that you can learn right now. The Bible tells us that there is only one God. He created everything. That means you, too! God made you so he can love you. And he wants you to love him back. If you know that, you know the most important thing of all!

My Bible Verse:

We know that there is only one God, the Father, who created everything, and we exist for him.

1 Corinthians 8:6, NLT

My Prayer:

Lord, I am here because of your love.
You're the only God in heaven above.

29 AUGUST

Just like Honey

How many honeybees do you see? There must be lots of honey inside the beehive! Have you ever tasted honey? Honey is very sweet. Most people like things that taste sweet. The Bible says that pleasant words are sweet like honey. People like to hear nice, pleasant words. No one likes to hear angry or grumpy words. Pleasant words are kind words. Pleasant words make people feel happy. What pleasant words can you say today?

My Bible Verse:

Pleasant words are like honey. They are sweet to the spirit and bring healing to the body.
Proverbs 16:24, NIrV

My Prayer:

Help me, Lord, with the words I say. I want to be pleasant and kind today.

Follow the Leader

30
AUGUST

Can you help Jack count the ladybugs? See if you can find which one is the leader. Have you ever played follow-the-leader? Everyone who follows has to do everything the leader does. So you always want to be sure to follow a good leader. God is the very best leader. He sent his Son, Jesus, to show us how to follow him and please him. The more we follow God, the more we will be like him.

My Bible Verse:
Follow God's example in everything you do, because you are his dear children.
Ephesians 5:1, NLT

My Prayer:
I want to follow where you lead,
To say kind words and do good deeds.

31 AUGUST

Have Faith

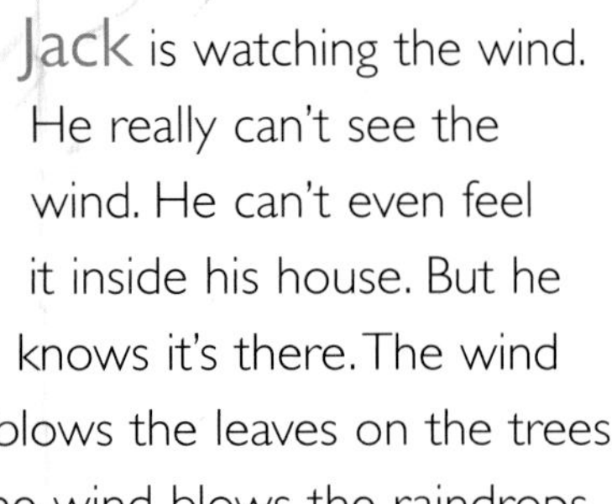

Jack is watching the wind. He really can't see the wind. He can't even feel it inside his house. But he knows it's there. The wind blows the leaves on the trees. The wind blows the raindrops against the window. Having faith means that you believe in something you can't see or feel. You can't see God, but you know he made the stars and the sky and the rivers. So you have faith that God is real. You know it's true.

My Bible Verse:
Faith means knowing that something is real even if we do not see it. Hebrews 11:1, ICB

My Prayer:
Oh, God, you're real—I know it's true. I want to put my faith in you.

September

1 SEPTEMBER

Don't Fall

Do you think Kaitlyn is strong enough to hold on to Jack so he doesn't fall? We need to be careful not to fall, because we don't want to get hurt. But we also need to be careful not to do bad things. If we do, that will hurt us too. When we disobey our parents or say words that are not kind, we need God's help. He is strong. And he can hold on to us to keep us from doing bad things.

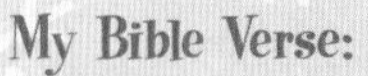

My Bible Verse:

God is strong and can help you not to fall. Jude 24, ICB

My Prayer:

Dear God, I know that you are strong. Keep me from doing whatever is wrong.

Naming the Animals

2
SEPTEMBER

What animal is this? It's a lion! Whenever you see an animal, you know what to call it, don't you? If you see a dog, you call it a dog. If you see a cat, you call it a cat. Did you ever give a special name to your own dog or cat or teddy bear? It's fun to think of names for animals. But someone had to think of what to call every kind of animal in the whole world. God gave that job to Adam, the very first man. Adam named the lions, tigers, horses, cows, owls, frogs, lizards, and everything else!

My Bible Verse:
[Adam] gave names to all the livestock, birds, and wild animals.
Genesis 2:20, NLT

My Prayer:
Thank you for animals all around,
From birds in the air to bugs on the ground.

3
SEPTEMBER

Nighttime Song

Zoë is playing a song for her animal friends so they can go to sleep. Do you like to sing songs? Did you know that a song can be a prayer? Singing a song for God is just like praying. Maybe you know a song you can sing as a bedtime prayer. Whether you say the words or sing them, God loves to hear your prayers.

My Bible Verse:
At night I have a song, and
I pray to my living God.
Psalm 42:8, ICB

My Prayer:
(To the tune of "Jesus Loves Me")
Jesus, Jesus, I love you.
Yes, I really, really do. (repeat first 2 lines)
I love you, Jesus. (sing 3 times)
I really, really do!

Get Wisdom

4
SEPTEMBER

Jack can't wait until he can read these big books. But he can look at some books right now. What kinds of books will help Jack know what God wants him to do? How about Bible storybooks? And books like the one we're reading, with Bible verses and prayers. The Bible gives us wisdom so we'll know how God wants us to live. Do you want to have wisdom? Just pray and ask God to give it to you. He will help you listen to his words from the Bible.

My Bible Verse:

If you need wisdom—if you want to know what God wants you to do—ask him.
James 1:5, NLT

My Prayer:

Dear God, my wisdom comes from you. Help me to please you in all that I do.

5 SEPTEMBER

A Good Life

Zoë is thinking about God's promises in the Bible. One promise is to give us a long and happy life. But God doesn't promise that to everyone. He promises a good life to those who honor their parents. You honor your parents when you love them and are kind to them and obey them. Do you honor your parents? If you do, then God promises to give you a long, good life.

My Bible Verse:
Honor your father and mother . . . that it may go well with you and that you may enjoy long life on the earth. Ephesians 6:2-3, NIV

My Prayer:
Lord, you promise a life that is good
If I honor my parents the way that
I should.

God Knows

6 SEPTEMBER

Jack has a question for God. What do you think he is wondering about? Maybe he wonders what he will be someday. Do you wonder what is going to happen tomorrow or next week? People wonder about a lot of things. But only God knows the answers. He knows what will happen tomorrow. He knows what will happen next week. And he knows what will happen when you grow up. God knows everything that is going to happen every day. And since God knows, you don't have to worry about it.

My Bible Verse:

I am God, and there is no one else like me. Only I can tell you what is going to happen even before it happens.
Isaiah 46:9-10, NLT

My Prayer:

Lord, you know what tomorrow will bring.
Help me to trust you for everything.

7
SEPTEMBER

Love Your Neighbor

Jack's legs are shorter than Kaitlyn's, and he's tired. Kaitlyn loves Jack, so she is helping him. If you love your family and your friends, you'll help them whenever you can. God wants you to love others as much as you love yourself. It's easy to show love to yourself because you know what you need. Sometimes it's hard to know how to love someone else. But God can show you how. And he can give you enough love to share with everyone.

My Bible Verse:
Love your neighbor as yourself.
Galatians 5:14, NLT

My Prayer:
When loving others is hard to do,
Help me to get more love from you.

Like Eagles

8
SEPTEMBER

Parker and Zoë are pretending they're going to fly like a bird. Have you ever seen a big bird called an eagle? Eagles are very strong. They can fly higher than other birds. The Bible says we can be strong like eagles. When we have problems, we sometimes get tired and feel sad. But if we ask God to help us, he makes us feel better. He gives us new strength so we can feel happy and be strong like eagles.

My Bible Verse:

Those who trust in the Lord will receive new strength. They will fly as high as eagles. They will run and not get tired. They will walk and not grow weak. Isaiah 40:31, NIrV

My Prayer:

Help me, dear God, when I'm
weak and sad.
Give me new strength so I can
be glad.

9

SEPTEMBER

Forever and Ever

Kaitlyn is pretending to be a queen! Have you ever pretended to be a king or queen? It's fun to pretend that you are one of the most important people in the world. There have been many kings in many countries. But God is the only one who has been the King since the very beginning.

He is the King of the whole world! The Lord our God will always be the King.

My Bible Verse:

The Lord is king forever and ever! Psalm 10:16, NLT

My Prayer:

Dear God, you rule over everything. Forever and ever, you will be King.

Sea Creatures

10
SEPTEMBER

Kaitlyn is holding Jack so he can explore the ocean. He is finding friendly fish and pretty seashells. He even sees plants growing on the bottom! When God created the world, he put many living things in the ocean—from tiny snails to giant whales. Wouldn't it be fun to see everything that lives in the ocean? If you don't live by the ocean, maybe you can explore the ocean through books.

My Bible Verse:
God said, "Let the water be filled with living things."
Genesis 1:20, ICB

My Prayer:
Thank you for creatures that live in the sea.
All that you've made is amazing to me!

11 SEPTEMBER

Shine like Stars

Zoë and Kaitlyn are looking at the stars. Do you like to look at the stars? They are far, far away. But because they shine so brightly, we can see them. God wants you to shine like a star. He wants people to see how much you love Jesus and how kind you are. He wants people to enjoy being around you. Do you think you can be a shining star for Jesus?

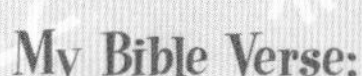

My Bible Verse:

Among the people of the world you shine like stars in the heavens.
Philippians 2:15, NIrV

My Prayer:

Jesus, I want to shine like a star
And show your love both near and far.

Run from Evil

12

SEPTEMBER

Jack saw something he'd like, but it doesn't belong to him. So he's running away from it. Have you ever wanted to take something that wasn't yours? Have you ever felt like telling a lie or disobeying your parents? Everyone feels like doing wrong things sometimes. But the Bible says to run from evil. When you feel like doing something wrong—don't do it! Pray to God. He will help you run from evil and do something good instead.

My Bible Verse:

Do what is good and run from evil. Amos 5:14, NLT

My Prayer:

If I want to do something bad today,
Help me to quickly run away.

13 SEPTEMBER

God Hears You

Parker just helped a grasshopper that was caught under a branch. Parker lifted up the branch so the grasshopper could hop away. Just like that little grasshopper, people get in trouble too. But when we do, we can call out to God. He will always hear our prayers and help us. He will rescue us just like Parker rescued the grasshopper.

My Bible Verse:

The Lord hears his people when they call to him for help. He rescues them from all their troubles. Psalm 34:17, NLT

My Prayer:

*Whether my troubles are big or small,
I know you'll hear me whenever I call.*

Even at Night

14

SEPTEMBER

Is it day or night in this picture? During the day God helps you with all you do. He helps you do your chores. And he helps you be kind to everyone. But at night God helps you too. Whether you're roasting marshmallows with your friends or getting ready for bed, God is there. He will protect you and guide you all through the night.

My Bible Verse:

I praise the Lord because he guides me. Even at night, I feel his leading. Psalm 16:7, ICB

My Prayer:

Even at night, Lord, you are there
To guide me and keep me in your care.

15 SEPTEMBER

It Is Good

God created the world in six days. He started by creating day and night. Then he made the sky and the land and the sea. God made trees and plants. He put the sun, moon, and stars in the sky. God put fish in the sea, birds in the air, and animals on the land. Finally, God created a man and a woman. When God looked at everything he had made, he saw that it was all very good. What are some of your favorite things that God made? You can say thank you to God for making everything good.

My Bible Verse:
God saw all that he had made, and it was very good.
Genesis 1:31, NIV

My Prayer:
Dear God, your creation is perfect for me.
Thank you for making all that I see.

Friends Forever

16 SEPTEMBER

Kaitlyn and her friends love being together. They want to be friends forever! God is like that too. No matter what happens, God will always love you. God wants you to love him, too, so he can be your friend forever. Sometimes friends move away and you can't talk to them. But God will never leave you. You'll always be able to pray to him every day.

My Bible Verse:

Nothing at all can ever separate us from God's love because of what Christ Jesus our Lord has done. Romans 8:39, NIrV

My Prayer:

I'm glad you'll always be my friend. Your love for me will never end.

17
SEPTEMBER

East to West

Have you ever seen the sun rise in the east in the morning and set in the west at night? If you have, then you know that east and west are far, far apart. Do you think you can measure the distance between east and west? Nope! It's impossible! The Bible tells us that God forgives us for the bad things we do when we tell him we are sorry. And do you know what? God takes those bad sins far, far away from us—as far as the east is from the west!

My Bible Verse:

He has taken our sins away from us as far as the east is from west.
Psalm 103:12, ICB

My Prayer:

Forgive me for bad things I've done today.
Thank you for taking my sins far away.

Feeling Tired?

18 SEPTEMBER

Poor Jack doesn't feel well. His friends hope he will feel better soon. Being sick makes you feel so tired you want to sleep all day. You feel too weak to run and play. But God can heal your body and make you strong. If you are tired for any reason, just ask God to give you his strength. You can ask your friends to pray for you too.

My Bible Verse:
He gives strength to those who are tired. He gives power to those who are weak. Isaiah 40:29, NIrV

My Prayer:
When I feel sick and tired all day,
Give me strength, Lord, to run
and play.

19
SEPTEMBER

Planting Seeds

Have you ever planted seeds? If you plant flower seeds, you'll grow flowers. If you plant pumpkin seeds, you'll grow pumpkins. Whatever you put into the ground, that's what will grow. The same thing is true with the way you act. If you plant kind words and helpful actions because you love God, you'll grow into a kind, helpful person who will live with God forever!

My Bible Verse:
Those who live to please the Spirit will harvest everlasting life from the Spirit.
Galatians 6:8, NLT

My Prayer:
I want to grow in my love for you,
To please you, Lord, in all that I do.

God's Masterpiece

20

SEPTEMBER

Zoë is painting a beautiful picture of herself. It's a masterpiece! That means she's doing an excellent job. When God created you, he did an excellent job too. The Bible says that you are a masterpiece. God did his very best when he made you. Now he wants you to do your very best for him. How can you do your best for God? What helpful, kind, and loving things can you do?

My Bible Verse:

We are God's masterpiece. He has created us anew in Christ Jesus, so that we can do the good things he planned for us long ago.
Ephesians 2:10, NLT

My Prayer:

Lord, you made me the way that I am. Help me to do the best that I can.

21

SEPTEMBER

Healthy Bodies

Kaitlyn is running to get some good exercise. When you exercise, your body becomes healthy and strong. It's important to take care of your body, because God made it. But it's also important to say and do things that please God. He is happy when you work hard to show your love for him. The best way to do that is to obey him. If you obey him, you become godly. That means you do good things the way God does. Then you're healthy inside and out!

My Bible Verse:

Training the body has some value. But being godly has value in every way. 1 Timothy 4:8, NIrV

My Prayer:

God, I will love you and try to obey,
So I can be healthy in every way.

Delight in God

22
SEPTEMBER

Zoë is making a wish and pulling off flower petals. She thinks that doing this may tell her if her wish will come true. "Yes, it will. No, it won't," says Zoë. Have you ever wished for something? The Bible says that if we delight in God, he will give us what we wish for. To delight in God means to love him more than anything else in the whole world. It means to be happy about obeying him. It means to enjoy praying to God. If you do all of that, God will help you to wish for the things HE wishes for you. And he will give you those things.

My Bible Verse:

Find your delight in the Lord.
Then he will give you everything
your heart really wants.
Psalm 37:4, NIrV

My Prayer:

Oh, Lord, I want to love you more
Than anyone I have loved before.

23 SEPTEMBER

Work with a Smile

Kaitlyn is working hard to clean up her room. Why do you think she is smiling? Maybe she is happy because she knows that when she works hard, God is happy. When you do your chores, you do them because your parents ask you to. But you can also work hard as a way to show God that you love him. And that will put a smile on your face!

My Bible Verse:

Work hard and cheerfully at whatever you do, as though you were working for the Lord.
Colossians 3:23, NLT

My Prayer:

Whenever I have to work for a while,
Help me to work with a happy smile.

A Lazy Day

24
SEPTEMBER

Zoë had a lazy day. She enjoyed a picnic in the shade. And she took an afternoon nap. Now it's time to go home. Zoë knows that God watches over her—even on a lazy day. God watches over you too. Whether you go on a picnic or take a nap or stay at home, God promises to watch over you all the time. And because God faithfully keeps all of his promises, you can be sure he'll do it!

My Bible Verse:
The Lord . . . watches over those who put their hope in his faithful love. Psalm 33:18, NIrV

My Prayer:
Lord, I know you will always be Faithfully watching over me.

25
SEPTEMBER

Talk about Them

Who do you think Jack is talking to? What might he be talking about? God tells us to talk about his rules, called commandments. God tells us not to lie or steal. He tells us not to say bad words. He tells us to honor our parents. He tells us to love and worship him. And he tells us to love our neighbors. When we learn God's commandments, we need to talk about them with our friends and family. That helps us to understand and obey them.

My Bible Verse:

The commandments I give you today must be in your hearts. . . . Talk about them when you are at home. Deuteronomy 6:6-7, NIrV

My Prayer:

I want to obey the commandments
you give.
They help me know how you want
me to live.

The Sea Is His

26 SEPTEMBER

Zoë likes the sound of ocean waves. Can you make a splish-splash sound? The ocean is so big that you can't see across to the other side. Sometimes an ocean is called a sea. People can dig a hole in the ground and fill it with water to make a little pond or a lake. But only God could create a big ocean or sea. That's why every ocean belongs to him.

My Bible Verse:
The sea belongs to him, for he made it.
Psalm 95:5, NLT

My Prayer:
Dear God, you made the great big sea.
And though it's yours, you share it with me.

27 SEPTEMBER

Branches with Fruit

What is Jack picking from the tree? Fruit grows on the branches of a fruit tree. If the branches are cut off from the tree, the fruit cannot grow. Jesus says that when we love and obey him, we are like branches that grow fruit. Jesus can help us do good things. But if we don't love Jesus, we are like branches that have been cut from the tree. What kind of branch do you want to be?

My Bible Verse:

I am the vine; you are the branches. Those who remain in me, and I in them, will produce much fruit. For apart from me you can do nothing.
John 15:5, NLT

My Prayer:

Jesus, please help me to always be
Like a branch that grows good fruit
on a tree.

Treasures in Heaven

28
SEPTEMBER

Zoë and Parker are finding lots of old things in a treasure chest. But these things won't last forever. Clothes get holes and fall apart. Toys get rusty or break. The Bible says it's more important to save up treasures in heaven. Whenever we do something for God, it becomes a treasure in heaven! We can save up treasures in heaven by telling others about Jesus or by being helpful or by sharing.

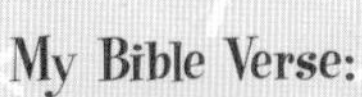

Store up for yourselves treasures in heaven.
Matthew 6:20, NIV

My Prayer:
My treasures on earth will soon be past.
But, Lord, what I do for you will last.

29

SEPTEMBER

You're in Charge

God put people in charge of taking care of his creation. How is Zoë helping to do that? We can also feed the animals. We can water the flowers. And we can keep lakes and rivers clean. We show God we're thankful for the things he made when we take good care of them. What are some other ways to take care of God's creation?

My Bible Verse:

You put us in charge of everything you made, giving us authority over all things.
Psalm 8:6, NLT

My Prayer:

Thank you, Lord, for trusting me
To care for animals, lakes, and trees.

You Are Priceless!

Kaitlyn is painting a picture of herself. It doesn't cost much to paint a picture, but Kaitlyn's mom and dad will think it is very special. That's because they love her so much. Some things cost a lot of money, like computers and TVs. But there are some things that money can't buy, like pictures and smiles and love. Those things are priceless. God says you are priceless too. He loves you very much. You are worth more to God than anything else in the whole wide world!

My Bible Verse:

You are priceless to me.
I love you and honor you.
Isaiah 43:4, NIrV

My Prayer:

Lord, you love me through and through.
I'm glad that I am priceless to you.

October

Stand Firm

1
OCTOBER

Smack! How far did Parker hit that baseball? To hit a ball, you need to stand firm and know exactly what you want to do. The Bible tells us to know exactly what we believe about Jesus. Do you believe that Jesus loves you and that he is God's Son? If you stand firm in what you believe, no one can change your mind. You know that what you believe is true!

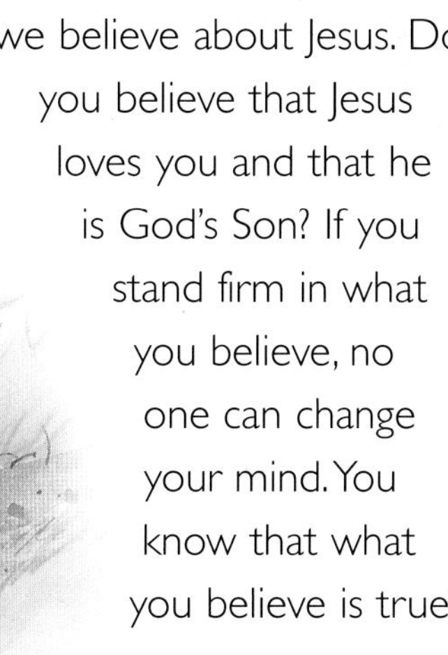

My Bible Verse:
Stand firm in what you believe.
1 Peter 5:9, NIrV

My Prayer:
Help me, Jesus, to always stand firm,
To accept and believe the things
that I learn.

2 OCTOBER

Be Careful!

Kaitlyn and her friends are being careful. They are waiting for the right time to cross the street. Do your parents ever tell you to be careful? They love you. They want you to be safe. God tells us in the Bible to be careful to do what's right. He wants you to be wise and obey your parents. They'll help you do what is right. God wants you to be careful because he loves you.

My Bible Verse:

Be very careful, then, how you live—not as unwise but as wise.
Ephesians 5:15, NIV

My Prayer:

I'll try to be careful; I'll try to obey
And do what is right every day.

Good Job!

3 OCTOBER

"Good job, Zoë!" says Kaitlyn. Zoë zipped her jacket all by herself. Can you try to do that? Good job! Kaitlyn is proud of Zoë and is encouraging her. She wants Zoë to feel good about what she has learned to do. God wants us to encourage others. Especially when they do something that pleases him. Do you think you can encourage someone today?

My Bible Verse:

Let everything you say be good and helpful, so that your words will be an encouragement to those who hear them.
Ephesians 4:29, NLT

My Prayer:

Help me to offer words of cheer
That other people need to hear.

4 OCTOBER

Even the Birds

How many bluebirds do you see? Do you know what they're doing? Birds like to sing! Who made the birds? Yes, God did! God made everything that lives. He made all the animals and birds and fish—and people, too! The Bible says that every living thing should sing praises to God. We should praise God because he's wonderful and because he loves us. You can sing songs to him just like the birds that chirp every morning!

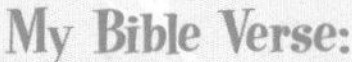

My Bible Verse:

Let everything that lives sing praises to the Lord!
Psalm 150:6, NLT

My Prayer:

Lord, I will praise you with my words
And sing to you like the little birds.

Be Led by the Spirit

5
OCTOBER

Zoë saw a hungry little lamb. Zoë's mother gave her a bottle of milk so she could feed the lamb. Zoë knew it would be a good thing to do. If you love God, God's Holy Spirit will lead you. He will help you see good things that you can do. Then it's up to you to do them! Maybe God's Spirit will lead you to play with your little brother or sister. Maybe he will lead you to help your mom. What else might he lead you to do?

My Bible Verse:
The true children of God are those who let God's Spirit lead them. Romans 8:14, ICB

My Prayer:
I want your Spirit to let me see
When others can use some help
from me.

6

OCTOBER

Without Wings

Kaitlyn, Zoë, and Parker are wearing wings. They are pretending to be angels. Do you ever pretend that you have wings and can fly? The Bible says that someday we really will fly though the air! Jesus will come back from heaven. When he comes, we will meet him in the sky and he will take us to be with him. And do you know what? You won't even need wings!

My Bible Verse:

We will be taken up in the clouds to meet the Lord in the air.
1 Thessalonians 4:17, ICB

My Prayer:

Dear Jesus, someday I'm going to fly
To meet you way up in the sky.

All the Same

7
OCTOBER

Zoë's paper dolls all look the same. But do you and your friends all look the same? How are you different? Maybe some of you are tall and some are short. Some of you have yellow hair and some have black or brown or red hair. God made us to look very different from each other. But do you know what? The Bible says that all of us who love Jesus are God's children! Jesus loves each of us exactly the same. And that's how we should love each other!

My Bible Verse:
You are all the same in Christ Jesus. Galatians 3:28, ICB

My Prayer:
Jesus, when we believe in your name,
We're one big family—all the same.

8
OCTOBER

Treating Others Right

Do you like to play "London Bridge" with your friends? What else do you play? When you play with your friends, it is important to treat them right. Taking turns and sharing are good ways to treat your friends right. The Bible says to treat others the way that you want to be treated. If you are kind to others, they will be kind to you. That's the way it works!

My Bible Verse:
Do to others as you would have them do to you. Luke 6:31, NIV

My Prayer:
Lord, help me be kind and
thoughtful too,
Then I will love others the
way that you do.

Ask God

Zoë is thanking God for cookies and for animal friends. She is also asking God to keep Parker safe as he goes to visit his grandparents. Who can you ask God to help? It's important to pray for your family and friends. Maybe you know some people who are sick or sad or lonely. You can ask God to help each one. And when God answers your prayers, remember to say thank you!

My Bible Verse:

Ask God for the things people need, and be thankful to him.
1 Timothy 2:1, ICB

My Prayer:

There are many who need your help today.
Thank you for hearing me when I pray.

10 OCTOBER

A Sweet Smell

What is Kaitlyn letting her cat sniff? Do you like the sweet smell of a flower? People like to be around flowers because they smell so nice. Do you want people to like being around you? If you really love Jesus, then you will want to act like Jesus did. You will be kind and helpful. Then people will like being around you. That's because you will be like a sweet-smelling flower.

My Bible Verse:

Our offering to Christ is this: We are the sweet smell of Christ among those who are being saved and among those who are being lost.
2 Corinthians 2:15, ICB

My Prayer:

Help me, Jesus, to be like you
So others will enjoy me too.

Naming the Stars

11
OCTOBER

Jack and Parker are putting stars on the bedroom ceiling. If you could name a star, what would you name it? God made all the stars that you see in the sky. He made more stars that are so far away you can't see them! He tells the stars to come out every night. And he has given each star its very own name. If God cares that much about stars, just think how much he cares about you!

The Lord causes the stars to come out at night one by one. He gives each one of them a name. Isaiah 40:26, NIrV

My Prayer:

Oh, Lord, you put the stars up high
To shine so bright in the nighttime sky.

12
OCTOBER

Helping Each Other

A little bird's nest fell down. Can you see how upset the mother bird looks? Zoë is trying to help by picking up the nest. Do you ever have days when everything seems to go wrong? How do you feel when your parents or friends help you? It's always nice to have help with your troubles, isn't it? Troubles go away faster when we help each other. Who can you help today?

My Bible Verse:
Help each other with your troubles. Galatians 6:2, ICB

My Prayer:
When someone needs a helping hand,
I want to help as best as I can.

Joyful Hearts

13 OCTOBER

Parker and Kaitlyn have joyful hearts. What do you think makes them happy inside and out? You can have a joyful heart if you think about all the great things God does for you. God is your Father in heaven. He loves you very much. He takes care of you and gives you what you need. God promises never to leave you. And God always keeps his promises. Now that can put joy in anyone's heart!

My Bible Verse:
The Lord . . . keeps us safe. Our hearts are full of joy because of him. Psalm 33:20-21, NIrV

My Prayer:
Oh, Lord, I want a joyful heart.
Thinking of you is where I'll start.

14

OCTOBER

God Hears Your Cry

Poor Jack! He fell down and hurt his knee. Kaitlyn heard him crying. She's going to carry Jack until he feels better. Do you ever get hurt? Does your mom come to help you when she hears you crying? God hears you when you cry too. He can make your bumps and scratches heal up. He'll take the hurt away. And he will help you to not feel so sad. He'll keep helping you until you feel lots better.

My Bible Verse:

I waited patiently for the Lord to help me, and he turned to me and heard my cry.

Psalm 40:1, NLT

My Prayer:

Dear God, I know you hear my cry,
And you can help from heaven on high.

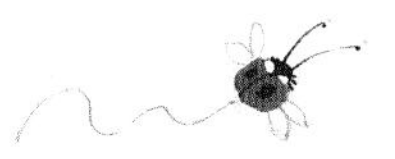

Love, Love, Love!

15
OCTOBER

Kaitlyn is looking at herself in a mirror and thinking about how much God loves her. God's love is greater than any love in the whole world. He loves you more than you'll ever understand. If God loves you so much, don't you think you should love him back? The Bible says to love God with everything that's within you. Hold your arms out wide like Kaitlyn is doing. Then tell God, "I love you this much!"

My Bible Verse:

Love the Lord your God with all your heart and with all your soul and with all your strength.
Deuteronomy 6:5, NIV

My Prayer:

Dear God, I pray that you will see I love you with every part of me.

16 OCTOBER

Strong and Steady

Kaitlyn just threw a ball. She needs to be strong and steady so she won't fall. We need to be strong and steady for other things too, like riding a bike or climbing monkey bars. And God wants us to be strong and steady in the way we live. When we believe in God and obey him, he helps us to be strong. If we do wrong things, it's like falling down. But God helps us get up again. He holds on to us to keep us steady. Then we're able to keep on obeying him.

My Bible Verse:

God himself will build you up again. He will make you strong and steady. 1 Peter 5:10, NIrV

My Prayer:

Help me, Lord, to be steady and strong
And live for you the whole day long.

Over and Over

17 OCTOBER

Kaitlyn is reading her favorite Bible story. She reads it almost every night. Do you have a favorite story that you read or listen to over and over again? When we really like a story, we never get tired of it. That's how God wants us to feel about his words in the Bible. He wants each of us to enjoy his teachings so much that we think about them all the time.

My Bible Verse:

He loves the Lord's teachings. He thinks about those teachings day and night. Psalm 1:2, ICB

My Prayer:

I love your words and what they say. I think about them every day.

18 OCTOBER

God's Promise

Parker is thinking about a very special promise God made a long time ago. God said that he would send his Holy Spirit to anyone who believes in Jesus. The Holy Spirit helps us every day. He helps us know what is right and wrong. He helps us know how to please God. God's promise is for grown-ups and children. It's for people all over the world, including you!

My Bible Verse:
You will receive the gift of the Holy Spirit. This promise is for . . . everyone the Lord our God calls to himself. Acts 2:38-39, ICB

My Prayer:
Your promise, God, is for everyone
Who believes in Jesus Christ,
your Son.

A Clean Heart

19

OCTOBER

Zoë is taking a bubble bath. She is washing her hair and her body so she will be clean. But did you know we need to wash our hearts, too? You can't wash your heart with soap and water. Only God can wash your heart. When you tell God you are sorry for your sins, he washes your heart. Then your heart is clean on the inside—just like you are on the outside after a bubble bath!

My Bible Verse:
Create in me a clean heart, O God. Psalm 51:10, NLT

My Prayer:
Lord, please wash my heart today,
And make my sins go far away.

20 OCTOBER

Lots of Prayers

Do you pray at bedtime like Kaitlyn? What if two or three other kids pray when you pray? That's not a problem for God. He can hear lots of prayers—all at the same time! God does not have a body like we do. God is a spirit. So he can do things that we can't do. Even if more than a thousand people pray at one time, God can hear them all!

My Bible Verse:
God is Spirit, so those who worship him must worship in spirit and in truth.
John 4:24, NLT

My Prayer:
Lord, you can hear many prayers
at a time,
So I know you will always listen
to mine.

Too Many Problems

21 OCTOBER

Zoë has too many problems today. What do you think she's upset about? Do you ever have problems like that? Everyone has troubles now and then. But God is always there to help. He will protect you if you are afraid. He will help you trust him so you can be strong. Whenever you have problems, talk to God. He'll help your problems get better.

My Bible Verse:

God is our protection and our strength. He always helps in times of trouble. Psalm 46:1, ICB

My Prayer:

If too many problems come along,
Please protect me and help me be strong.

22

OCTOBER

Add Goodness

Jack and Kaitlyn picked some apples. Jack is sharing one of them with a little lamb. Everyone will be happy to hear what he did. When you do good things, like sharing your toys, people will see that you love Jesus. Maybe you know some people who don't believe in Jesus. If you do good things, they may want to know more about Jesus because of you.

My Bible Verse:

You should try very hard to add goodness to your faith.
2 Peter 1:5, NIrV

My Prayer:

Jesus, I'll do good things for you
So others will want to know you too.

Under His Wings

23
OCTOBER

Have you ever seen a mother bird sitting on her nest? She is protecting her babies. She spreads her wings over them to keep them safe and warm. The Bible says God is like that too. He is our Father in heaven. And he cares about everyone in his family. He wants to protect us and keep us safe. It's good to be God's child. He loves you very much. And he will care for you. Just like a mother bird cares for her babies.

My Bible Verse:
He will protect you like a bird spreading its wings over its young. Psalm 91:4, ICB

My Prayer:
Lord, when I'm safely under your wings, I know you'll protect me, whatever life brings.

24 OCTOBER

Let's Make Music!

Zoë and Jack are marching in a parade. Can you see what they are playing? It's exciting to hear the drums when the bands march by in a parade! Music is a wonderful gift from God. He created us so we can sing and play instruments. We can use music to say thank you to God. We can praise God with songs that tell how great he is. Praising God with music will make you feel happy, even on a gloomy day!

My Bible Verse:

Let us come to him and give him thanks. Let us praise him with music and song.
Psalm 95:2, NIrV

My Prayer:

Lord, I will praise you with music and song,
And then I'll be happy the whole day long.

Peaceful Friends

25
OCTOBER

Zoë wants her animal friends to get along together. She doesn't want them to fight. She wants them to be happy and peaceful. So she's giving them all a ride in her wagon. They don't have to fight about who gets to ride first. Do you try to be kind and helpful to others? Do you try not to fight? If you work to keep everyone happy and peaceful, God will help you be happy and peaceful too.

My Bible Verse:

God blesses those who work for peace, for they will be called the children of God.
Matthew 5:9, NLT

My Prayer:

I'll help my friends who want
to fight
By showing them how to do
what's right.

26 OCTOBER

Getting Along

Do these animals love each other? How can you tell? They like being together, don't they? Do you like being with your brother or sister? Do you get along with your family and friends? God wants us to live together in harmony. He wants us to get along with each other. When we love each other, we enjoy doing things together. We live in harmony. Sometimes it's hard to get along with the people we live with. But God's love will help you love everyone the way he wants you to.

My Bible Verse:
Love is what binds us all together in perfect harmony.
Colossians 3:14, NLT

My Prayer:
Thanks for loving my family and me
So we can live in harmony.

Teach What Is Right

27
OCTOBER

Kaitlyn wants to be a teacher someday. Do you think she will be a good teacher? One of the most important things to teach others is to love God. When people love and obey God, they learn what a kind, helpful friend he is. They want to talk to him, and they end their prayers by saying "Amen," the word on Kaitlyn's chalkboard. There are many good things to teach. But teaching others to love God is the best.

My Bible Verse:
I will teach you what is good and right. I Samuel 12:23, ICB

My Prayer:
Lord, I must learn many things
about you
And then teach others to love
you too.

28 OCTOBER

Special Clothes

Jack and Kaitlyn put on white nightgowns just for fun. Do you think they will wear them all day? Do you have a favorite daytime outfit? Clothes can keep us warm on cold days and cool on warm days. The Bible talks about some special clothes. It says to clothe yourself with Jesus. That means you should try to act like Jesus in everything you do. When you do that, you'll always be wearing the right outfit!

My Bible Verse:
Clothe yourselves with the Lord Jesus Christ. Romans 13:14, ICB

My Prayer:
Jesus, please help me every day
To act like you in every way.

What to Choose?

29 OCTOBER

Parker and his friends are looking at some toys. They can't decide which one to choose. Have you ever had a hard time choosing something? Did you know that God makes choices too? He chose you to be a part of his family. But God didn't have a hard time choosing you. He loved you and chose you a long time ago, even before you were born.

My Bible Verse:

He chose us from the beginning, and all things happen just as he decided long ago.
Ephesians 1:11, NLT

My Prayer:

Thank you, dear God, for choosing me
To be a part of your family.

30 OCTOBER

Real Angels

Kaitlyn likes her angel doll. She takes it with her lots of places. It reminds her that God's angels are all around her. Since we can't see real angels, it's easy to forget that they are here. But God tells us in the Bible that he sends his angels to those who believe in him. Even though we can't see them, God's angels are all around us to protect us day and night.

My Bible Verse:

The Lord saves those who fear him. His angel camps around them. Psalm 34:7, ICB

My Prayer:

Thank you for sending your angels here. Though I can't see them, I know they're near.

Love in the Morning

The sun is shining in Jack's window and the birds are singing. He's even getting a kiss from his dog! When you wake up in the morning and see the sunshine, say thank you to God. When you hear the birds singing in the morning, say thank you to God. And when someone wakes you up with a kiss, say thank you to God. These are some of the ways that God shows his love for you.

My Bible Verse:
In the morning let me hear about your faithful love.
Psalm 143:8, NIrV

My Prayer:
Dear God, when I wake up each day,
Thanks for your love, which comes
my way.

November

You Are Important!

1 NOVEMBER

Kaitlyn likes to be a helper. She cleans her room and feeds her cat. Those are important things to do! Even though you are young, you can do many important things. Do you pick up your toys? Do you put your clothes away? Do you bring your dirty dishes to the sink? What other important things can you do? You do many important things. That means YOU are important too—especially to God!

My Bible Verse:

You are young, but do not let anyone treat you as if you were not important.
1 Timothy 4:12, ICB

My Prayer:

Show me, dear God, how I can do Important things for others too.

2 NOVEMBER

A Little Secret

Zoë likes making her own snack. She has a little piece of celery with some peanut butter, and she's putting a few raisins on top. That doesn't sound like much, but Zoë thinks it's wonderful! Everything we have comes from God. We should be thankful for big things, like our family and our home. But we should also be happy for little things, like snacks. Then we'll know the secret of always being happy.

My Bible Verse:
I have learned the secret of being happy at any time.
Philippians 4:12, ICB

My Prayer:
Thank you, dear God, for all that you give.
I'll try to be happy each day that I live.

The Right Path

3

NOVEMBER

Jack and Zoë are taking a walk. They know the right path to take so they won't get lost. Have you ever gotten lost? It's important to stay on the right path. When we need to know the right way to act, it's like needing to find the right path. God can help you choose the right things to do. If you learn Bible verses and pray, God will help you stay on the right path and do the right things.

My Bible Verse:

Show me the path where I should walk, O Lord; point out the right road for me to follow.
Psalm 25:4, NLT

My Prayer:

I'll learn from you, Jesus, so I can know
The right things to do and the right
way to go.

4 NOVEMBER

Get Rid of the Dirt!

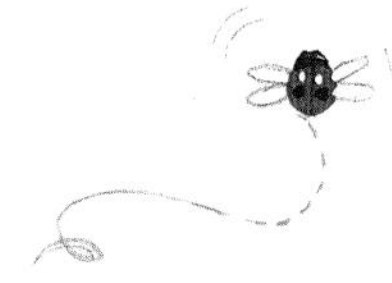

Jack and Zoë are dirty from playing in the mud. But the good news is that they can get rid of the dirt by washing it off. Did you know that when we do bad things, our sin is like dirt on the inside? But God gets rid of the dirt by forgiving us when we tell him we're sorry. So now you know how to get rid of the dirt on the outside and the inside!

My Bible Verse:

If we confess our sins, he will forgive our sins. We can trust God. He does what is right. He will make us clean from all the wrongs we have done.
1 John 1:9, ICB

My Prayer:

I'm sorry, Lord, for all of my sin. Forgive me and make me clean within.

Happy or Grumpy?

5
NOVEMBER

Zoë is waking up happy after a sleepover. But Kaitlyn is still tired. She's feeling a little grumpy. Do you ever wake up feeling grumpy? If you start your day by praising God, it will help you to be happy. You can stretch out your arms and say, "Thank you, God, for a wonderful new day!" After saying thank you to God, you can't possibly be grumpy!

My Bible Verse:
Happy are the people who know how to praise you.
Psalm 89:15, ICB

My Prayer:
Thank you, dear God, for every new day,
For happy smiles and prayers to say.

6 NOVEMBER

Being Silly

Look at how happy Kaitlyn and Parker are. Isn't it nice when you can be silly and have fun? Isn't it nice when you don't have to worry about anything? If you believe that God sent his Son, Jesus, to be your friend, you know that God loves you very much. He takes care of your problems. And he watches over you. You can be silly and have fun because God takes care of everything for you!

My Bible Verse:
I pray that God, who gives you hope, will keep you happy and full of peace as you believe in him. Romans 15:13, NLT

My Prayer:
Dear Lord, you love me and care for me too,
So I can leave all my worries with you.

Be a Friend to Everyone

7 NOVEMBER

What animals do you see in this picture? Which animal is big? Which one is small? The cat could act important and chase the little mouse away, but that's not what's happening. Have you ever tried to chase away a little brother or sister? God wants you to be a friend to everyone. He loves us all the same. We should try to be more like God. We should love old people and babies. We should love tall people and short people. We should love everyone the same.

My Bible Verse:

Be willing to be a friend of people who aren't considered important.

Romans 12:16, NIrV

My Prayer:

Help me to be a friend to all,

No matter if they are big or small.

8

NOVEMBER

Calm Down!

Do you think Kaitlyn looks mad? If her dog gives her a big kiss, maybe she won't be angry anymore. Do your friends ever get mad? Maybe you could give a hug to an angry friend. Or you might say something kind to that person. Hugs and quiet, gentle words can help an angry person to calm down. Sometimes people who are mad just need to know that someone loves them.

My Bible Verse:

A gentle answer will calm a person's anger. Proverbs 15:1, ICB

My Prayer:

Dear God, if someone is mad today,
Please help me to know what words to say.

Summer and Fall

Kaitlyn likes to rake leaves in the fall. She doesn't rake leaves in the summer when it's hot. And she doesn't rake them in the winter when it's cold and snowy. The fall season always comes after the summer season. And winter always follows fall. Can you say the order of the seasons? God promises that the seasons will always follow each other in the right order.

My Bible Verse:

As long as the earth remains, there will be springtime and harvest, cold and heat, winter and summer, day and night.

Genesis 8:22, NLT

My Prayer:

Thank you, Lord, for summer and fall
And winter and spring—you made them all!

10 NOVEMBER

Accept One Another

Can you tell who is under the big nose and mustache and glasses? It's Jack! And who has big eyeballs on top of her head? It's Zoë! Some people wear real glasses to help them see. And noses come in all shapes and sizes! People look different from one another. But Jesus wants you to accept other people and be their friend, even if they are different from you. He wants you to accept them just the way they are. That's how Jesus accepts you!

My Bible Verse:
Accept each other just as Christ has accepted you.
Romans 15:7, NLT

My Prayer:
At home or away, or wherever I may be,
I'll try to love others the way you love me.

Listen and Learn

11
NOVEMBER

Who do you think the dog is listening to on the phone? Jack likes to listen to his grandma. When you listen to your parents and grandparents and teachers, you learn many things. If you're wise, you'll never stop learning. You can learn from books, and you can learn by going to school. And you can always learn by listening to other people. Ask God to help you listen and learn.

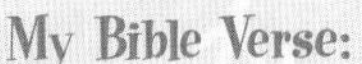

My Bible Verse:

Let wise people listen and
add to what they have learned.
Proverbs 1:5, NIrV

My Prayer:

Help me to listen to what others say
So I can keep learning, day after day.

12 NOVEMBER

Be Humble

Do you know what it means to be proud? People who are proud think they are better than others. God doesn't like it when we are proud. He wants us to be humble. People who are humble are willing to help others. They are willing to do the jobs that others don't want to do. Do you think Kaitlyn is being proud or humble? God's favorite people are those who are humble instead of proud.

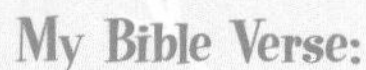

My Bible Verse:

God sets himself against the proud, but he shows favor to the humble. James 4:6, NLT

My Prayer:

Help me, Jesus, so I can see
That being humble is what I should be.

A Special Name

13 NOVEMBER

Parker and his friends are finding letters to spell their names. Do you know how to spell your name? Names are important. They have special meanings. Do you know what your name means? The most special name is the name Jesus. This name means Savior. Only Jesus, the Son of God, can have a name that means Savior. He's the only one who can save us from our sins.

My Bible Verse:

You are to name him Jesus, for he will save his people from their sins.
Matthew 1:21, NLT

My Prayer:

Jesus, you have a special name.
You're my Savior—that's why you came.

14 NOVEMBER

Without Words

Do you see the book with no words? Guess what? You can say thank you to God without words! God likes to hear the words of your thank-you prayers. But there is another way you can say thank you to God. God tells us in the Bible how he wants us to live. When you obey God and do what is right, it's like saying thank you to him. And you don't even need words!

My Bible Verse:

I will thank you by living as I should! Psalm 119:7, NLT

My Prayer:

Dear Lord, I will say thank you to you
By doing the things you want me to do.

A Comforting Promise

15
NOVEMBER

Parker is sad because his plant is dying. Maybe if he gets another plant, he will feel better. Do you ever feel sad? Everyone feels sad now and then. But God is always there to make us feel better. He promises to comfort us with his love. And God's love is the best love in the whole world!

My Bible Verse:
Comfort me with your love,
as you promised me.
Psalm 119:76, ICB

My Prayer:
Thank you, God, for sending your love
To comfort me from heaven above.

16 NOVEMBER

Kindness Counts

Kaitlyn is teaching Jack and Zoë how to count. Do you know how to count? It's important to learn how to count. But it's also important to learn how to treat others. God wants us to do good things for others. He wants us to be fair. We shouldn't be nice to one person and mean to another. The next time you practice counting, count the number of friends you have. Then try to be kind to all of them.

My Bible Verse:

Learn to do good. Be fair to other people. Isaiah 1:17, ICB

My Prayer:

Help me, Lord, to be kind and fair
To all of my friends as we play
and share.

All I Need

17 NOVEMBER

Kaitlyn is thirsty and wants some milk to drink. Her refrigerator has lots of good food in it. Does your refrigerator have good food in it? How about your closet—do you have some clothes in it? The Bible says if we have food and clothes, we have what we need. And we should be happy. If you have what you need, remember to say thank you to God.

My Bible Verse:

If we have food and clothing, we will be happy with that.
I Timothy 6:8, NIrV

My Prayer:

Lord, since you give me clothes and food,
I know I should be in a happy mood.

18
NOVEMBER

Pray for Leaders

Kaitlyn is thanking God for her food. She's also praying for some people. Who are some people you pray for? Do you pray for your grandpa or grandma? Do you pray for your friends? Those are all special people to pray for. But God also wants you to pray for your leaders, because they make important decisions. The next time you pray, ask God to help your leaders make the right decisions.

My Bible Verse:
You should pray for kings and for all who have authority.
1 Timothy 2:2, ICB

My Prayer:
I'll pray for my leaders day and night.
I'll ask you to help them do what is right.

The Earth Obeys

19 NOVEMBER

Do you see wind? Do you see rain? Long ago, God created the world, and everything happened the way he wanted it to. When God said, "Let there be light!" there was light. When God said, "Let there be fish!" many fish swam in the water. Today, God can still give commands to the world he made. If he wants the rain to stop, it will stop. If he wants the wind to blow, it will blow. Only God can give a command that will stop a storm.

My Bible Verse:
He gives a command to the earth, and it quickly obeys him.
Psalm 147:15, ICB

My Prayer:
Dear God, whenever you give a command,
All things obey you on water and land.

20 NOVEMBER

Not Even Angels

What are these girls pretending to be? Yes, angels! There are many angels in heaven. Jesus is coming back to earth from heaven someday. He wants to take us to live with him. It's going to be a very special day! But do you know what? No one knows when that day will be. Not even the angels! If you love and obey God, you will be ready when Jesus comes back.

My Bible Verse:
No one knows the day or hour . . . not even the angels.
Mark 13:32, NLT

My Prayer:
Jesus, how special the day will be
When you come back for your family!

Brighter and Brighter

21
NOVEMBER

Kaitlyn is waking up to the morning sun. Have you ever watched the sky get brighter and brighter as the sun rises higher? The Bible says that's what people who love God are like. They keep doing good things until everything around them seems brighter! Do you want to brighten up a room? Do you want everyone around you to feel happy? Then keep doing good things and let your light shine!

My Bible Verse:
The way of the good person is like the light of dawn. It grows brighter and brighter until it is full daylight.
Proverbs 4:18, ICB

My Prayer:
I'll try to do good and turn everything bright,
Making others happy with my shining light.

22 NOVEMBER

Remember and Obey

Jack and Kaitlyn are pretending they are a mom and dad. Have you ever done that? Someday you just might be a parent! When you grow up, you will remember many good things your parents taught you about God. Then you can teach them to your children. And someday they will teach them to their children. Can you think of something you've already learned about God from your dad or mom?

My Bible Verse:

Keep your father's commands.
Don't forget your mother's teaching.
Proverbs 6:20, ICB

My Prayer:

Thank you for parents who teach me your way.
Help me remember their words and obey.

Give Thanks

23
NOVEMBER

Parker is ready to eat a great big meal. He is thankful for all of the good food! Do you ever have a big dinner with your family? Do you remember to thank God for all of the good things he does for you? God loves you so much. God takes good care of you. He gives you many things. Remember to give thanks to God for everything he does for you every day.

My Bible Verse:

Give thanks to the Lord, because he is good. His faithful love continues forever. Psalm 118:1, NIrV

My Prayer:

Thank you, Lord, for the gifts
you send
And for your love that will
never end.

24 NOVEMBER

God Made the Stars

Kaitlyn opened her window so she could see the beautiful sky. She can see the stars that form the Big Dipper. She likes to look at the twinkling stars. Do you like to look at the stars? When you see them in the sky, you know that only God could have created them. What other things do you see at night that God made?

My Bible Verse:

I look at the heavens, which you made with your hands. I see the moon and stars, which you created. Psalm 8:3, ICB

My Prayer:

Lord, you made each twinkling star
To show how powerful you are.

How Do You Act?

25
NOVEMBER

Zoë is following some ducks going for a walk. "Quack! Quack! Quack!" says Zoë. Have you ever acted like a duck? It's fun to act like something else. But how do you act when you are being yourself? If you are polite and kind, people will see that and be pleased. If you are crabby and mean, people will see that, too. And they won't be pleased. It's important to act in a way that shows you love Jesus.

My Bible Verse:

Even a child is known by his behavior. His actions show if he is innocent and good.
Proverbs 20:11, ICB

My Prayer:

Help me, Lord, to act in a way
That makes you like what I do and say.

26 NOVEMBER

A Sweet Reward

Jack has a yummy ice cream cone that he can't wait to eat. It's his reward for finishing a big job his parents asked him to do. What kinds of rewards do you like to receive? We should always try to be helpful and obey, because that's how God wants us to live. The Bible says God will reward us for the good things we do. We're not sure exactly what those rewards will be. But if they are from God, we know they will be the best!

My Bible Verse:

You reward people for the way they live and for what they do.
Jeremiah 32:19, ICB

My Prayer:

Jesus, I'll do my best for you,
And enjoy your reward for what I do.

Don't Be Troubled

27

NOVEMBER

"Be careful, Jack!" says Kaitlyn. She is worried that Jack might fall. He's trying to help her cat. It climbed up the tree and couldn't get down. Have you ever worried that someone might get hurt? There are many things that can trouble us or make us sad. But Jesus wants us to trust him. He is able to take care of anything that troubles us.

My Bible Verse:

Don't be troubled. You trust God, now trust in me. John 14:1, NLT

My Prayer:

When I am troubled, I know that
I must
Turn to you, dear Jesus, the one
that I trust.

28 NOVEMBER

Bow Down and Worship

Kaitlyn is talking to Jesus, God's Son, who came to earth as a baby. When he grew up, he did many miracles. Those were special things that only God's Son could do, like making sick people better. Then Jesus died on the cross for our sins so all who believe in him can go to heaven. He came back to life. Now he lives in heaven. Jesus is greater than any king. He is so special that all who hear his name must bow down and worship him, just like Kaitlyn.

My Bible Verse:

At the name of Jesus every knee will bow, in heaven and on earth and under the earth.

Philippians 2:10, NLT

My Prayer:

Jesus, it was for me that you came.
I want to worship your holy name.

A Good Hiding Place

29
NOVEMBER

Kaitlyn's cat found a good hiding place. Do you think anyone will find her? Do you have a place where you like to hide for a little while? Do you ever snuggle under the bedcovers or hide behind a big chair? The Bible says that God is like a hiding place. He will protect us from troubles so that troubles cannot even find us.

My Bible Verse:
You are my hiding place;
you protect me from trouble.
Psalm 32:7, NLT

My Prayer:
Dear God, you're like a hiding place,
For you protect me and keep me safe.

30 NOVEMBER

One More Thing

Kaitlyn had many important things to do today. But before she goes to sleep, she wants to do one more important thing. She wants to talk to God and tell him she loves him. She wants to thank him for helping her today. Before you go to sleep tonight, what important thing can you do? What will you tell God? Will you thank God for helping you with everything you did today?

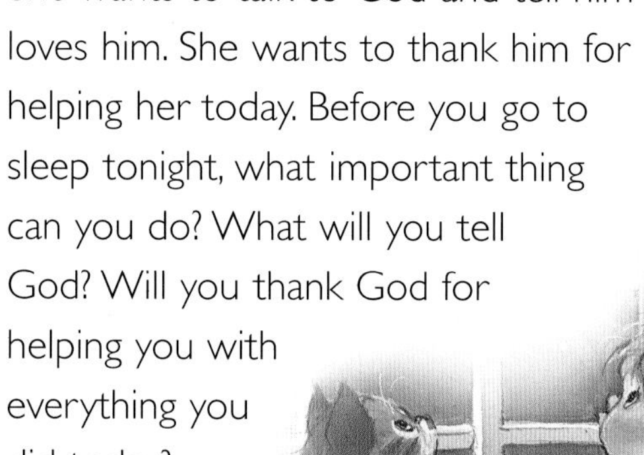

My Bible Verse:
*On my bed I remember you;
I think of you through the . . .
night. Psalm 63:6, NIV*

My Prayer:
*I know you hear me as I pray.
Thank you, Lord, for helping me today.*

December

1

DECEMBER

Millions of Stars

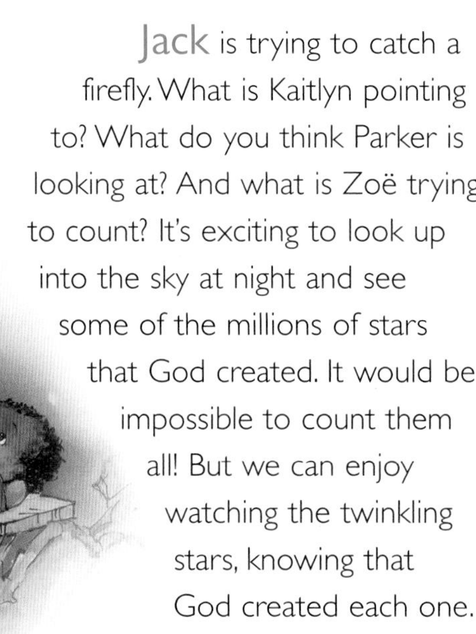

Jack is trying to catch a firefly. What is Kaitlyn pointing to? What do you think Parker is looking at? And what is Zoë trying to count? It's exciting to look up into the sky at night and see some of the millions of stars that God created. It would be impossible to count them all! But we can enjoy watching the twinkling stars, knowing that God created each one.

My Bible Verse:

In the beginning you made the earth. And your hands made the skies. Psalm 102:25, ICB

My Prayer:

Dear God, when I see each twinkling star,
It shows me how wonderful you are.

Pay Attention

2 DECEMBER

Jack does not want to go to bed. Kaitlyn is telling him that he should. If Jack doesn't go to bed, he will be tired and grumpy in the morning. Do you think Jack will listen to Kaitlyn? Does your mom or dad ever tell you to do something that you don't want to do? Your parents know what is best for you, because God helps them to be wise. They're happy when you pay attention and do what they say!

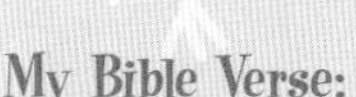

My Bible Verse:

Pay attention and listen to the sayings of those who are wise.
Proverbs 22:17, NIrV

My Prayer:

Dear God, I'm still a very small size,
So help me listen to those who are wise.

3 DECEMBER

What Will Last?

Zoë feels sad because all the leaves have fallen off her favorite tree. Do you ever find leaves on the ground? When the weather gets cold, the leaves dry up and fall to the ground. Leaves and many other things don't last very long. But some things last forever. The Bible was written thousands of years ago, and it's still here so we can listen to it and learn from it! God's Word will never die. It will last forever.

My Bible Verse:
The grass withers and the flowers fall, but the word of our God stands forever.
Isaiah 40:8, NIV

My Prayer:
Dear Lord, we have your Word today.
I thank you that it is here to stay.

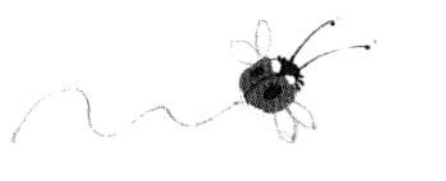

True Messages

4 DECEMBER

Kaitlyn made some angel wings to wear. Before the Bible was written, God would send angels to give special messages to people. The angel would tell the people not to be afraid. The angel would tell them what God was going to do. Everything that the angels said came true. One time an angel told Mary that she was going to be the mother of God's Son. Do you know who that baby was?

My Bible Verse:
The message God delivered through angels has always proved true. Hebrews 2:2, NLT

My Prayer:
Lord, when messages come from you, I know that they are always true.

5 DECEMBER

Happy Days

Kaitlyn and Zoë are having a happy day. They are reading stories and enjoying their animal friends. Do you like having happy days? The Bible says that we can be happy if we obey God. We know we're obeying God when we follow the rules in his Word, the Bible. When we do what God wants us to do, we please him. And we give ourselves many happy days.

My Bible Verse:

Happy are the people who . . . follow the Lord's teachings.
Psalm 119:1, ICB

My Prayer:

Help me, Lord, to follow your ways
So my life will be filled with happy days.

Giving to Others

6 DECEMBER

Kaitlyn worked hard all morning making a blueberry pie for her mom. She can hardly wait to see the happy look on her mom's face! Did you know that gifts don't have to come from a store? You can color a picture or make a card. Maybe someone can help you bake some cookies to give as a gift. God gives us so much. And he wants us to be happy to give gifts to others.

My Bible Verse:

I want you to be leaders also in the spirit of cheerful giving.
2 Corinthians 8:7, TLB

My Prayer:

All that I have, Lord, comes from you. I want to give gifts to others too.

7

DECEMBER

What Do You See?

Jack feels happy when he sees a special picture each morning. What do you see when you wake up? You can see many things that God has given you to show he is with you. You see your cozy bed and your clothes and pictures of your family. When you wake up, always thank God for everything you see. That's a great way to start each day. And someday you'll go to heaven and wake up to see God himself!

My Bible Verse:

When I wake up, I will be satisfied because I will see you. Psalm 17:15, NIrV

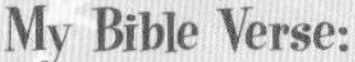

My Prayer:

Lord, I thank you for all that I see. My home and family are special to me.

Always God's Child

8
DECEMBER

Kaitlyn has lined up her dolls and animals to follow her as if they are her children. If you love Jesus, you are God's child. God promises to love you and give you everything you need. But do you know what? No matter how old you are, you will always be God's child. Even when you are all grown up, God will still love you and take care of you. Just as you follow him, his love will follow you!

My Bible Verse:
I am sure that your goodness and love will follow me all the days of my life. Psalm 23:6, NIrV

My Prayer:
Dear God, you will love me as long
as I live.
Thanks for the love and the goodness
you give.

9

DECEMBER

God Is Faithful

Kaitlyn promised to help Jack stand on his head. Is she being faithful and keeping her promise? Sometimes people forget to keep their promises. And sometimes they're not able to keep them. But God is faithful because he always CAN keep his promises, and he always WILL, no matter what. He will never change his mind. You can depend on God and trust him, no matter what!

My Bible Verse:

Let us hold firmly to the hope we claim to have. The One who promised is faithful.
Hebrews 10:23, NIrV

My Prayer:

Lord, you are faithful to do what you say.
I know I can trust you every day.

The Right Spot

10

DECEMBER

Zoë is trying to put the donkey's tail on the right spot. Do you think she can do it with a blindfold covering her eyes? It's hard to do things when we can't see. If we don't believe in God, it's just like having our eyes covered. But if you believe in God, he shows you what he wants you to do. He stays with you, just like someone who leads a blind person. And he always takes you to the right spot!

My Bible Verse:
You lead the people you have saved. Exodus 15:13, ICB

My Prayer:
Thank you, God, for helping me see. Thank you for guiding and leading me.

11

DECEMBER

How Much Longer?

Jack and Parker can hardly wait for their cake to be done. How much longer do you think it will be? Waiting teaches us to be patient. And patience helps us to trust God. He hears our prayers and knows what we need right away. But sometimes he wants us to wait for his answer. Waiting is hard. But good things are worth waiting for.

My Bible Verse:

Be still. Be patient. Wait for the Lord to act. Psalm 37:7, NIrV

My Prayer:

Lord, when waiting is hard to do,
I know I will get my patience from you.

Enjoy Life!

12
DECEMBER

When Parker is happy, he likes to jump up and down. Do you like to run and jump and play? What is your favorite thing to do? God wants us to have fun and to enjoy every day. Sometimes we have to rest or do our chores. But there should always be time for fun! The Bible says that even grown-ups should take time to have fun. The next time you are doing something really fun, remember to say thank you to God.

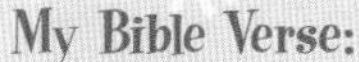

My Bible Verse:
If a person lives to be very old, let him rejoice in every day of life.
Ecclesiastes 11:8, TLB

My Prayer:
Thank you, God, for times of fun
And the joy you give to everyone.

13 DECEMBER

Good Gifts

Parker has lots of presents to buy. He wants to give one to each of his friends. He hopes he will get some presents too! Do you think he wants the car or the airplane? At Christmas people have fun giving gifts to one another. But the best gifts come from God. He gives us our friends and family. And he gives us his Son, Jesus, the most perfect gift of all.

My Bible Verse:

Every good and perfect gift is from God. It comes down from the Father. James 1:17, NIrV

My Prayer:

Father, you give such good gifts to me,
Like Jesus, my home, and my family.

Counting the Days

14 DECEMBER

Kaitlyn and Zoë are counting the days until Christmas. They can hardly wait! Do you know how many days it is until Christmas? On Christmas we celebrate Jesus' birthday. Before he was born, people waited and waited for him to come. When Jesus finally came, many people were excited and said thank you to God. But you don't have to wait until Christmas to thank God for Jesus. You can do it right now!

My Bible Verse:

We wait in hope for the Lord.
Psalm 33:20, NIV

My Prayer:

Thank you, God, for the gift of
your Son
And the love you give to everyone.

15 DECEMBER

Don't Do It!

Zoë is making some yummy treats for a Christmas party. Zoë wants to take a bite, but her mom told her to wait. Do you think Zoë will obey? We're tempted with many things, especially at Christmas. There are secrets to keep and presents to hide. And it's always hard to stay away from the candy and cookies! If you find it hard to obey your parents during the holidays, ask God to help you keep secrets and stay away from the treats.

My Bible Verse:
Keep us from falling into sin when we are tempted.
Matthew 6:13, NIrV

My Prayer:
Help me, Lord, when it's hard to obey. Help me to do what my parents say.

A Time to Rejoice

16 DECEMBER

Kaitlyn, Jack, and Zoë are decorating a Christmas tree. What kinds of ornaments do you hang on your tree? Do you put angels or stars on it? These ornaments have special meanings. The angels told shepherds that Jesus was born. And the star helped wise men find him. Some ornaments are just for fun. But all of them remind us that Christmas is a time to be happy and rejoice.

My Bible Verse:

I will rejoice in the Lord! I will be joyful in the God of my salvation.
Habakkuk 3:18, NLT

My Prayer:

Jesus, I'll say it with a loud voice—
Christmas is a time to rejoice!

17 DECEMBER

Filled with Love

Uh-oh! Parker was stringing some popcorn, but someone got hungry! Parker is going to have to find more popcorn. Sometimes things happen that can make us mad or upset. But God doesn't want us to be angry. He wants our hearts to be filled with his love. When we are filled with God's love, the little things won't bother us so much. Does Parker look angry? Or does he look like he is filled with God's love?

My Bible Verse:
May the Lord fill your hearts with God's love.
2 Thessalonians 3:5, NIrV

My Prayer:
Dear God, I want my friends to see I have your love inside of me.

Working for Fun

18 DECEMBER

Kaitlyn, Jack, and Parker are making Christmas cookies. It will take a lot of work. But when the cookies are done, they will get a reward—they'll have cookies to eat together! The Bible says that hard work often brings happy rewards. When the kids eat their cookies, do you think they will be happy they worked so hard?

My Bible Verse:

Many good things come from what a man says. And the work of his hands rewards him.
Proverbs 12:14, NIrV

My Prayer:

Lord, when there's work that needs to be done,
Help me remember that work can be fun.

19
DECEMBER

Receive God's Promise

A long time ago God promised that he would send a Savior to save people from their sins. People who believed that the Savior was coming had faith that God would keep his promise. God's promise came true when Jesus was born. Do you see the star that reminds Kaitlyn of Jesus' birth? Today God promises that all who believe in Jesus will be saved from their sins. You can receive God's promise by believing in Jesus.

My Bible Verse:

People receive God's promise by having faith. Romans 4:16, ICB

My Prayer:

Jesus, I know God's promise is true. I can be saved by believing in you.

Worship and Sing

20
DECEMBER

The children are dressed like angels for the Christmas play. They are going to worship God by singing praises to him. When we worship God, it shows God that we love and honor him for being so great. Even the angels worship God and give him praise. On the first Christmas they praised God for sending his Son, Jesus. But you can worship God any day of the week, all year long.

My Bible Verse:

Let all the angels of God worship him. Hebrews 1:6, NLT

My Prayer:

I will worship you, Lord, with a joyful song,
Not only at Christmas, but all year long.

21
DECEMBER

Ring the Bells!

Jack and Zoë are listening to the church bells ring. Have you ever heard church bells? Churches ring their bells to let people know it's time to come to the church. Sometimes churches ring their bells for a special program during the Christmas season. So if you listen carefully, you might hear bells ringing! And you'll know it's time for everyone to praise God for his Son, Jesus.

My Bible Verse:

The nations will praise you forever and ever. Psalm 45:17, NLT

My Prayer:

Thank you for bells that ring loud
and clear,
So people will worship from far
and near.

Lots of Gifts!

22 DECEMBER

What do you think Jack is excited about? It's also exciting to think about the day when Jesus will come back to earth and take us to heaven. But until Jesus comes back, God promises to give us gifts every day. He gives you food and clothes. He gives you your home and your friends and your family. God gives you so many gifts, they could never fit under a Christmas tree!

My Bible Verse:
You have every gift from God while you wait for our Lord Jesus Christ to come again.
1 Corinthians 1:7, ICB

My Prayer:
Thank you, Lord, for the gifts you send.
Christmas will never have to end!

23 DECEMBER

Happy Shepherds

What story is Kaitlyn reading? The Christmas story is one of the best Bible stories! Do you know who told the shepherds about baby Jesus? Just think how happy the shepherds must have been when they found the baby. On the way back to their sheep, they praised God and thanked him for letting them see his Son. We can thank God for Jesus too.

My Bible Verse:

The shepherds went back to their sheep, praising God and thanking him for everything that they had seen and heard. It was just as the angel had told them.

Luke 2:20, ICB

My Prayer:

Dear God, I thank you for Jesus,
your Son.
The Christmas story is the very
best one!

Looking for Jesus

24
DECEMBER

Can you find the three wise men that Jack sees? These men came from far away to worship baby Jesus. We don't have to travel far to find Jesus. We can read all about him in the Bible. And we can talk to him wherever we are. That's because Jesus grew up and went back to heaven. Now he can always hear our prayers. Doesn't that make Christmas special?

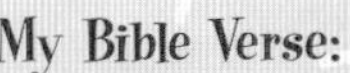

My Bible Verse:

Some wise men . . . asked, "Where is the baby who was born to be the king of the Jews? We saw his star in the east. We came to worship him."
Matthew 2:1-2, ICB

My Prayer:

Thank you, Lord, that I can see
You're always very close to me.

25
DECEMBER

Whose Birthday Is It?

It's Christmas morning! What do you think Kaitlyn and Jack will find under the tree? Do they both have a birthday today? No, it's Jesus' birthday! God sent his Son, Jesus, from heaven to earth. Mary and Joseph placed baby Jesus in a manger filled with hay. Jesus grew up to be our Savior. His birthday is the most important birthday of the whole year!

My Bible Verse:

Today in the town of David a Savior has been born to you; he is Christ the Lord.
Luke 2:11, NIV

My Prayer:

Thank you, Jesus, for coming today,
And for taking all my sins far away.

Obey with a Smile

26
DECEMBER

Zoë has been playing with her Christmas presents. Now it's time for bed. She would rather stay up a little longer. But Zoë knows it's best to obey. When you obey your parents, God is happy because you are doing what he wants. When you obey your parents, they are happy because you are doing what they want. And since everyone is happy, it should put a smile on your face too!

My Bible Verse:
Children, obey your parents in everything, for this pleases the Lord. Colossians 3:20, NIV

My Prayer:
I want to please you night and day.
Help me to try my best to obey.

27
DECEMBER

Win or Lose

Parker and Jack are having a snowball fight. Each boy hopes he will win! Do you like to win when you play games? Everyone likes to win. But when you play games, everyone loses now and then. Did you know there is something you can never lose? You can never lose God's love. No matter who may be against you, God will always be on your side.

My Bible Verse:

If God is with us, then no one can defeat us. Romans 8:31, ICB

My Prayer:

Dear God, I want to share this news: Your love is something I'll never lose.

Always Light

28 DECEMBER

It is dark outside, and Kaitlyn is sound asleep. In the morning when Kaitlyn wakes up, it will be light again. On the earth it is dark at night and light during the day. But in heaven, it never gets dark. That is because Jesus is there. Jesus is called the Light of the World. So wherever he is, it is always light.

My Bible Verse:

Even the darkness is not dark to you. The night is as light as the day.
Psalm 139:12, ICB

My Prayer:

Dear Lord, in heaven you shine
your light,
No matter if it is day or night.

29 DECEMBER

Outdoor Fun

Zoë and Kaitlyn like to play outdoors. What are they doing today? Do you like to play outdoors? When you play with your friends or your brother or sister, it's important to be kind and to share. When you are filled with God's love, God will help you to treat others the way that you should. You can ask God to fill you with his love every day so your playtime will be lots of fun.

My Bible Verse:

We thank God because we have heard about the . . . love you have for all of God's people.
Colossians 1:4, ICB

My Prayer:

Lord, fill me with your love today
So I will please you as I play.

God's Peace

30 DECEMBER

Do you see how quiet and peaceful everything looks around these houses? If it were noisy all the time it would be hard to rest or even think! God fills our lives with peace when we trust and believe in him. We don't have to worry about anything because God takes care of everything. God's peace is so great that we can have peace and rest even when it's noisy!

My Bible Verse:
The peace that God gives is so great that we cannot understand it. Philippians 4:7, ICB

My Prayer:
When I'm resting in your care,
Lord, your peace is everywhere.

31 DECEMBER

Blessings All Year

On this last day of the year, some people get together with their family and friends for a New Year's Eve celebration. The end of the year is a good time to think about all the wonderful blessings that you have from God. Can you think of special ways that God blessed you and took care of you this year? As you celebrate the end of the year, remember to say thank you to God for his many blessings.

My Bible Verse:
The Lord . . . blesses the homes of those who do what is right.
Proverbs 3:33, NIrV

My Prayer:
Thank you, Lord, for times of cheer
And all your blessings throughout the year.

Books in the Little Blessings line

- *Prayers for Little Hearts*
- *Questions from Little Hearts*
- *Bedtime Stories and Prayers*
- *What Is God Like?*
- *Who Is Jesus?*
- *What about Heaven?*
- *Are Angels Real?*
- *What Is Prayer?*
- *Is God Always with Me?*
- *Why Is There a Cross?*
- *What Is the Bible?*
- *Who Made the World?*
- *The One Year Devotions for Preschoolers*
- *The One Year Devotions for Preschoolers 2*
- *God Loves You*
- *Thank You, God!*
- *Many-Colored Blessings*
- *Bed Time Blessings*
- *God Created Me!*
  A memory book of baby's first year

CP0216

About the Author

Crystal Bowman received a bachelor of arts degree in elementary education from Calvin College and studied early childhood development at the University of Michigan. A former preschool teacher, she loves writing for young children and is the author of numerous children's books. Crystal is a writer and speaker for MOPS (Mothers of Preschoolers) International and has written several books in the recently published MOPS picture-book series.

Besides writing books, Crystal enjoys being active in the local schools, speaking at authors' assemblies, and conducting poetry workshops. Her books of humorous poetry are favorites in the classroom as well as at literacy conferences.

Crystal and her husband live in Grand Rapids, Michigan, and have three grown children.

About the Illustrator

Elena has illustrated over 100 children's books during the past 15 years for publishers such as Scholastic, Reader's Digest Children's Publishing, Hampton-Brown, Wishing Well Books, Tommy Nelson, and Concordia Publishing House. She has also illustrated for corporate clients, including General Mills, the National Wildlife Federation, American Greetings Corporation, and Pepsi.

For several years she worked for American Greetings as an artist and art director and then as a contract freelance artist. During this time she was the lead artist for the Care Bears and Care Bear Cousins, providing finished art for product and third party licensees such as Bates Nightwear, Kenner, Parker Bros., and the William Carter Company.

She received her BFA from Kent State University, has two grown daughters, and resides in Madison, Connecticut, with her husband, Tom.